MW00668581

The Art of
SPOON CARVING
A Classic Craft for the Modern Kitchen

LORA S. IRISH

DOVER PUBLICATIONS
Garden City, New York

About the Author

Lora S. Irish is a nationally and internationally known artist and author who currently has twenty-five wood carving, pyrography, and craft pattern books in publication, including *Chip Carving 1* and *2*, *Classic Carving Patterns*, *Landscapes in Relief*, *Wildlife Carving in Relief*, *Great Book of Fairy Patterns*, *Great Book of Dragon Patterns*, *Great Book of Floral Patterns*, *Great Book of Tattoo Patterns*, *Easy and Elegant Copper Jewelry*, and *Wood Spirits and Green Men*. Twelve of the author's purebreed dog oil canvas paintings have been published as limited-edition fine art prints.

Working from their home studio, Lora and her husband and webmaster, Michael, are the owners of two websites: www.ArtDesignsStudio.com, which features Lora's digital arts and crafts patterns, and www.LSIrish.com, where she offers free online tutorials and projects.

Acknowledgments

I would like to extend my deepest appreciation to the team at Dover Publications who contributed to the creation of this book: Vanessa Putt, the book's acquisition editor; Gregory Koutrouby, the book's in-house editor; and Jennifer Becker, the book's designer; as well as Marie Zaczkiewicz, Design Manager, Fred Becker and Segundo Gutierrez, who performed the color correction for the book's images, and Susan Rattiner, Supervising Editor, Jim Miller, Editor, and Kathy Levine, Copy Editor/Proofreader, who carefully checked the pages for accuracy, consistency, and continuity.

Copyright

Copyright © 2017 by Lora S. Irish
All rights reserved.

Bibliographical Note

The Art of Spoon Carving: A Classic Craft for the Modern Kitchen is a new work, first published by Dover Publications in 2017.

International Standard Book Number

ISBN-13: 978-0-486-81349-3
ISBN-10: 0-486-81349-5

Manufactured in the United States by LSC Communications Book LLC
81349505   2021
www.doverpublications.com

Contents

Introduction

One of the first things I did when I began working on this book was to go to my kitchen spoon jar to look for common spoon bowl and handle shapes. Like many cooks, I have a large assortment of spoons, each made for a different purpose and use in the kitchen.

Among all the fancy modern spoons stood an old, blackened, broken-edge spoon that has survived nearly one and a half centuries of hard, loving use.

The tip of the spoon is charred where it was used to adjust the kindling in a wood stove or to push a hot griddle off the burner. The left side of the spoon bowl tip has been worn away, so I know that over the years the women who used this spoon were right-handed. The bowl is permanently stained in a black-brown tone from decades of use in creating those wonderful jars of blackberry jam and grandpa's mulberry wine.

This spoon belonged to my great-grandmother Elsie Burchnial Shay, wife of George L. Shay, born 1870 in Preston County, West Virginia—five years after the end of the American Civil War.

She used the spoon through WWI and the Great Depression. My grandmother used it to make her daughters dinner when her husband was helping to build the Panama Canal and again during WWII. It was still stirring my mother's starter batter for bread when man first walked on the moon and when she made cookies to send to my brother during the Vietnam War. And today it sits in my kitchen spoon jar, ready for the next batch of ham and black bean soup.

As I held that spoon, I thought of all the items that have come and gone through my life: expensive power tools that have been retired, furniture that was replaced, fine jewelry and store-bought treasures that are no longer in fashion.

They're long gone, but a simple wooden spoon—which around 1870 probably cost less than a penny—has survived and has been cherished by four generations of women. And it's still sitting in my spoon jar.

We will be using this beloved old spoon as a template so that you can learn how to carve your own wooden spoons that will become your family heritage treasures.

CHAPTER 1

Tools and Supplies

A traditional stirring spoon can be carved using a simple set of beginner's carving tools which includes two sizes of round gouges, a v-gouge, a straight chisel, and a skew chisel. Deeper-bowled spoons may need the addition of a wide-sweep gouge and bent round gouge.

So let's begin by taking a look at the tools and supplies used in wooden spoon carving.

Carving Sets

Wood-carving tool sets usually include several sizes of round gouge, a straight chisel, a skew chisel, and a v-gouge. The thickness of a tool's metal shaft and handle determine whether it is used with a leather mallet or hand held. Any of these three sets can be used for spoon carving.

Mallet-Carving Set

Left to right:
½" bent round gouge
⅜" straight round gouge
⁵⁄₁₆" straight round gouge
¾" curved edge, wide sweep gouge
¾" straight edged, wide sweep gouge
¼" 60 degree v-gouge

Hand-Carving Set

Left to right:
⁵⁄₁₆" deeply bent round gouge
⁵⁄₁₆" bent round gouge
⅜" straight round gouge
¼" 60 degree v-gouge
⅜" straight chisel
⅜" skew chisel

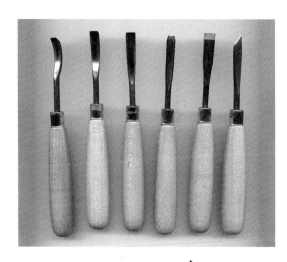

Japanese Hand-Carving Set

Left to right:
¼" straight chisel
⅜" skew chisel
¼" skew chisel
⁵⁄₁₆" straight chisel
¼" 90 degree v-gouge
³⁄₁₆" round gouge
¼" round gouge
⁵⁄₁₆" bull-nose chisel

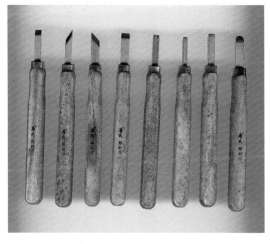

Round Gouges

Round gouges are defined by the width of the cutting arc and the shape or curve of the tool's body. Shown in the photo, left, is a bent round gouge. The tool body is curved to drop the cutting edge of the gouge inside the bowl area of your spoon. The cutting edge of this gouge is a tight, half-circle. Bent round gouges are excellent for the rough-out work for your spoon bowls.

Shown, lower left, is a wide sweep, straight-edged gouge. The cutting edge of this gouge has a long profile with a gentle arc. The wide open arc of the wide sweep is wonderful for smoothing spoon bowls. Wide sweep gouges are also called fish tail gouges.

Varieties of Round Gouges

Left to right:
Straight-edged wide sweep gouge
Curved-edge wide sweep gouge
Large straight round gouge
Large deeply bent round gouge
Medium deeply bent round gouge
Medium bent round gouge
Medium straight round gouge
Small straight round gouge

Bench Knife

Bench knives are available in a wide selection of blade lengths, from 2" to ¾" long. I prefer a short-bladed bench knife, which places my cutting hand closer to the wood, therefore giving me more control over the cutting stroke. Shown in the top left of this photo is a large chip-carving knife.

Draw Knife

The draw knife, shown center left, is a two-handled tool with a straight cutting edge. This particular draw knife is made specifically for wood carvers and has a 3" long semi-flexible blade. You can quickly reduce your carving block to your basic spoon shape using a draw knife.

Scoop Gouge

Shown center right, the scoop gouge, also called a hook knife, is a deeply curved gouge with the cutting edge on the side of the gouge instead of the front. Scoops are used to smooth the inside of the spoon bowl.

Carving Wood

Throughout the projects in this book I used basswood. This is a hardwood species that has tightly packed, fine-white grain and is easy to cut. Basswood is readily available in both boards and pre-cut blocks, which range from ⅜" to 2" thick by 4" to 12" long. Spoons can be carved out of any non-toxic wood species such as ash, birch, beech, and most fruit tree woods. I strongly suggest that you begin your spoon carving using basswood to learn the basic techniques, and then move on to other hard woods.

Sharpening Stones and Leather Strop

You will need a selection of sharpening tools in your carving kit. Shown in the photo, top left, is a 1000-grit coarse brown stone and 6000-grit fine white stone for establishing your knife edge bevel and sharpness. The two profiled leather boards, shown right top, are honing boards made specifically to fit the profile of your round gouges. The yellow honing compound is used on the leather strop to give an extremely smooth finish to your cutting edge. The newspaper is used last to brighten your tool.

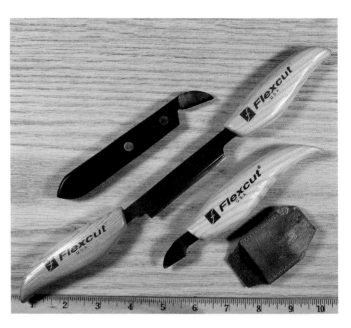

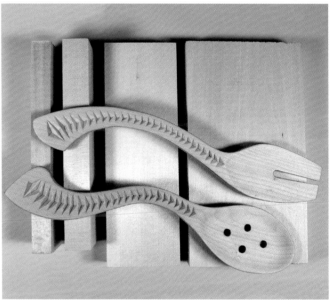

Carving Gloves

Safety is an important consideration with any wood-carving project. To protect your hands during the cutting of your spoons, there are several options that you can choose from. Carving gloves are manufactured in thick cotton, Kevlar, and in synthetic nylon with small plastic dots to aid in your gripping power. As with any glove they come in small, medium, and large sizes.

Thumb Guards

Thumb guards cover about two-thirds of your thumb or finger. I use one thumb guard on the thumb of my tool-holding hand and one on the index finger of my holding hand.

Terry-cloth Towel

I always have a large, thick terry-cloth towel on my lap during any carving session. The towel can be wrapped around the wood blank in my holding hand to protect my hand during hard or difficult push strokes. Also shown in the middle photo is a red, non-skid kitchen mat that I use with my draw knife and coping saw work to secure the wood blank with a clamp to the table. Scissors are used to create the lightweight cardboard spoon templates and a fine-point permanent marking pen is used to create guidelines of your rough-out.

Sandpaper and Rifflers

Sandpaper gives your wooden spoon that pristine smooth surface that is so comfortable to handle and hold while you are making up a batch of cookies. I use a range that includes 100-, 150-, 220- and 320-grit. Foam-core sanding blocks also come in a variety of grits and conform to the curve of your handles and bowl backs. A crumpled brown paper bag is the finest grit sanding medium that you can use. It will leave your wood nicely polished. I have several sizes of small dowel rods in my carving kit that I can wrap with sandpaper to smooth the inside edges of fork tines. You can also purchase small files and rifflers that come in a variety of shapes for sanding tight curved or angled spaces.

CHAPTER 2

Spoon Styles

here seems to be a spoon for every purpose in the kitchen, and the shape and depth of the spoon bowl is created to match that purpose. Along with spoons you can carve forks, ladles, spatulas, pie knives, icing knives, and even slotted spoons. Let's take a quick look at the classic spoon, fork, and knife shapes and their associated uses. As you work through the projects in this book, please remember that any project can quickly be adjusted or altered into a new and unique spoon by changing the bowl depth, length, and shape.

As an example, in the small photo at left, the bowl shapes of the saucepan spoon and relish spoon can easily be used with our Kitchen Companion handle project.

Traditional Spoon Styles

Medium-Sized Kitchen Spoons

The five spoons, shown at left, would have been common tools in our grandmother's kitchen. Medium kitchen spoons usually measure about 8" to 10" from the bowl tip to the handle end, with the bowl area being one-third the full length of the spoon.

Bottom photo, left to right: Dipping spoons have very round, deep bowls and the bowl size is adjusted to the common serving size of the food item. So you can have large dipping spoons for mashed potatoes and small dipping spoons for sauces.

The straight edge and bottom corner angle of this spoon exactly matches the straight walls of my sauce pans, allowing me to stir every area inside of the pan. This saucepan spoon is a must for making homemade candies or cheese sauces which tend to stick on the sides of the pan.

The center spoon is a dry ingredient or flour scoop. The high sides of the scoop keep the flour from slipping as you lift it from the bag. The second scoop, right of center, is a wet ingredient or butter scoop. This one has thinner and shorter walls near the edge of the scoop.

Our last common kitchen spoon is a wide scoop which can be used to move cookie dough from the mixing bowl to sheet pan or for serving stuffing, or flipping fried potato slices.

Large Kitchen Spoons

Batter spoons, shown at the top of page 9, have wide, flat bowls that can be used to roll and fold the dough or batter. This spoon's bowl is 3" wide but only ½" thick. Used as a shovel, this spoon style is used to lift and turn large amounts of stiff ingredients.

The open, deep bowl of the center spoon makes this one a soup or stirring spoon. This spoon can easily move large amounts of ingredients in your deepest pan.

Every farm house had a variation of this extra-wide, paddle-style spoon, used for making apple butter or rendering lard. Historically, this paddle would have a handle that could be several feet long to place the cook comfortably away from the outdoor fire and iron kettle.

All three of the above spoon styles traditionally measure between 12" and 14" from the bowl tip to the handle end.

Specialty Spoons

Every cook seems to have their favorite specialty spoon in the spoon jar on the stove. Let's take a moment and look at just a few.

Middle photo, top to bottom: Slotted spoons are common tools around the kitchen, but this slotted spoon with its single center hole is used to lift pickles or olives from the jar while draining away the juice.

The thumb print at the joint of the handle in this wooden blade lets you get a close grip on the knife as you spread the icing on your chocolate cake.

A bacon fork slides across the floor of your fry pan, lifting a strip of back while allowing the bacon fat to drain.

Folding stiffened egg whites into your next salmon soufflé batter is easy with this flat, long oval folding spoon. Note that in this spoon style the bowl area is one-half or longer than the total length of the spoon to give you lots of extra working room.

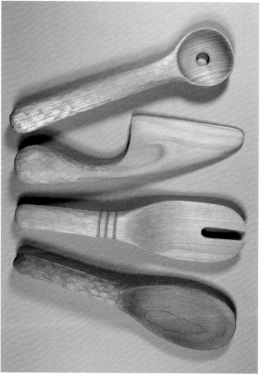

Bottom photo, top to bottom: World War I saw the introduction of mass-produced canned food for both the soldiers overseas and the home front. The top spoon in the bottom right photo comes directly from that era and was used to scoop the lard out of the new tins.

If you carve no other spoon than the second spoon in the bottom photo, every cook you know will praise your carving skills. This is an all-purpose oven rack spoon. The bowl shape can be used to fold, mix, or scoop. The handle is long enough to use in any sauce pan or deep cooking bowl. But it is the handle end that is most noteworthy. The hook on the handle is used to slip over a hot oven rack letting you pull it safely from the oven and the cut half-circle in the end goes against the outer rail of the rack so that you can push that hot rack back into the oven for more baking. A cook can do just about every job in the kitchen with this one spoon.

Large flat bowls and forks are the hallmark of salad serving spoons. Because these are lifting spoons, not stirring spoons, their handles easily accept decorative and curved style handles.

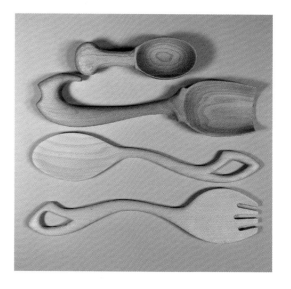

Mix & Match Carving

Once you learn the simple steps to carving your spoon bowl, fork tines, and handle styles you will be ready to create your own unique style of kitchen tools.

This fun set of barbeque and picnic spoons (above) was carved from ½" thick by 3" wide by 6" long basswood and took about one hour of carving for each utensil. Shallow and short, they are perfect to throw on your picnic table, ready to scoop up relish, pickles, and mustard.

Left & Right Handles

Curved spoon handles should be adapted to the individual user and the curvature determines which hand holds the spoon.

In the bottom photo, the two spoons on the left are shaped to fit left-handed chefs who move the spoon in a counter-clockwise motion.

The two spoons on the right are made for right-handed cooks. Any curved pattern can be reversed to make it either right- or left- handed.

CHAPTER 3

The Basic Process

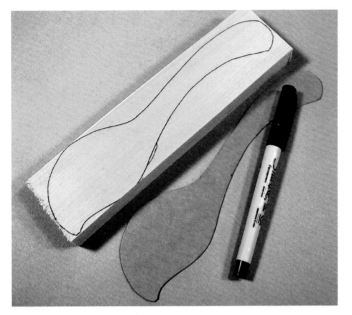

Transferring a Pattern

There are several easy methods to transfer your spoon pattern to your wooden blank.

Trace a copy of the pattern that you wish to use with tracing paper or tracing vellum and a pencil.

Graphite Paper Transfer

Center the vellum tracing pattern over the wood blank and tape one side of the paper to the wood to keep the paper from sliding. Graphite paper can be placed between the tracing pattern and the wood with the shiny side of the graphite paper against the wood. Follow the pattern lines with an ink pen. The graphite paper will leave a medium gray line on the wood.

Pencil Rubbing Transfer

You can blacken the back of your tracing pattern with a soft #4 to #6 pencil. Place the blackened side against the wood, centering the pattern. Trace along the pattern lines with an ink pen. This will leave a medium gray pencil line on your wood.

Template Transfer

I prefer to make a thin, chipboard or cardboard template for my spoon carvings.

Trace your spoon pattern to thin chipboard or cardboard. I find that the inside surface of cereal boxes or saltine cracker boxes work very well.

Cut the template free from the chipboard using scissors or your bench knife.

You can place the template directly onto the surface of your wood block and use a marking pen to trace along the outer edge of the template.

Templates can be used many times to create new spoons.

The bench knife is used to create the rough cutout for this double bowled tasting spoon carving.

Draw Knife Rough Cutting

The draw knife is a two handled, flexible straight blade that is used to rough shape your spoon blanks.

The blade has a chisel edge with the cutting edge placed face-up on the wood. It can be used for straight, concave, and convex cuts. The double-handle design gives you greater strength in your pull strokes, allowing you to remove large chips quickly. Grandma Shay's Spoon is rough-out cut using a draw knife.

Working with a Draw Knife

Here we will focus on using a draw knife to create the rough-out, carving support ears at the bowl and handle back joint, and cutting a deep, oval bowl.

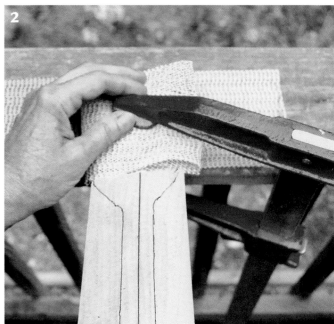

Setting up your draw knife session

Your wood blank needs to be clamped to a secure, stable work surface when you are using a draw knife. Choose a table, work surface, or as in the photo above, a strong section of porch railing that will not rock during your work session.

Cut two 12" squares of non-skid kitchen mat. Fold both pieces into quarters. Place one folded mat directly onto the work table surface. Position one end of your wood blank over the mat, with the main portion of wood extending towards you. Place the second piece of mat over the wood, and then apply the clamp.

1 A non-skid kitchen mat secures your wood to your table; it also protects the surface or face of the wood from clamp marks.

2 Because of the pressure on the wood with the pull stroke cut of a draw knife, you need to clamp your spoon blank to a strong, non-moving table.

3 Clamp the wood blank so that you have plenty of open space around your work area to allow you to easily adjust your hand position without readjusting the wood and clamp arrangement.

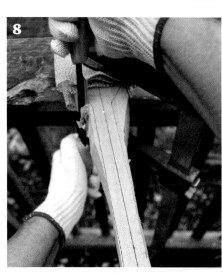

4 Place the draw knife blade against your wood with the beveled cutting edge up.

5 Use a two-handed grip, with one hand grasping each handle.

6 The cut is now made using an even pressure and a straight pull towards the end of the wood.

7 Readjust your clamp and wood as necessary to work new areas of the rough-out blank.

8 Tight curves are worked by first cutting the top half of the curve with a pull stroke—pulling the draw knife towards you.

9 The second half of the curve is cut using a push stroke, where the knife is reversed and pushed away from you.

10 Draw knife work not only creates the basic shape of the spoon in the rough-out stage, it can also be used to round over the handle, smooth the bowl and handle joint, and round over the back of the spoon.

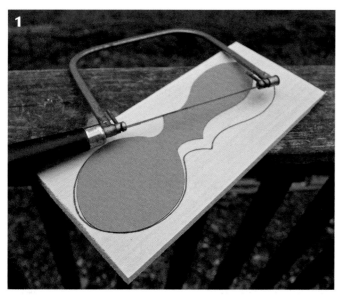

Using a Coping Saw

The coping saw is a great woodworking tool that you can use to quickly reduce your wood blank into a rough-cut spoon. The saw holds a scroll saw blade between two widely spaced arms, giving you plenty of room to cut tight, intricate curves along the edges of your spoon shape. This example features a Wedding Spoon.

1–2 Create a chipboard template of your spoon pattern. Lay the template onto your carving block, and using a marking pen, trace along the outer edge of the template.

Securing the wood blank

3–4 To use a coping saw for your rough cut steps you will need to secure your wood blank to a non-moving, non-rocking surface with plenty of open space to work the saw. Around my studio the most solid surface is my porch railing.

Because the wood blank for this project is thin stock, ½" thick, sandwich the wood blank between two scrap basswood boards. This gives the back side of the wood blank added strength during the cutting process and protects the wood blank from clamp marks.

Wrap a wide piece of non-skid kitchen mat around the outside of the wood sandwich. Place the sandwich on your secure surface and clamp into place.

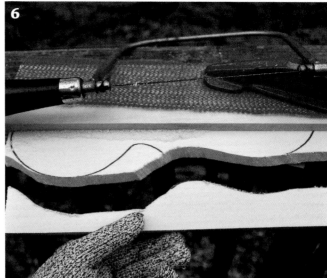

Cutting the rough shape

5 Coping saw blades come in a variety of tooth patterns, shapes, and spacing between teeth. A general, all-purpose cutting blade works well for most spoon projects.

At the end of each arm of your coping saw is a small, levered screw that can be loosened to open the hole that will hold the end of the saw blade. Set the blade into your coping saw with the blade teeth pointed down, or into the cut, as you work a push stroke.

6 The coping saw cuts on the down-stroke and is held at a right angle to your work surface to create as straight a cut wall as possible.

7 Cut away large sections of the excess wood around your spoon first. Then return to create new cuts to release the tighter angles and curves of the spoon.

8 When you have completed cutting one side of your wedding spoon, remove the spoon blank from the clamps and reposition the blank so that you can cut the second side.

The completed coping saw rough-cut spoon

9 Just as I do with my scroll saw and draw knife work, when I set up to use my coping saw I will do several spoon rough cuts during that session. The coping saw is so efficient that often it takes longer to set it up than it takes to cut the spoon.

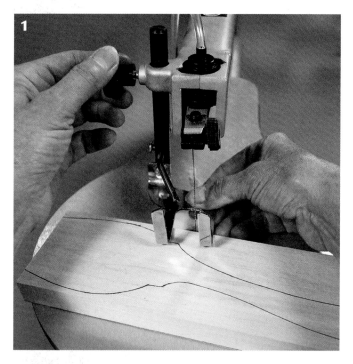

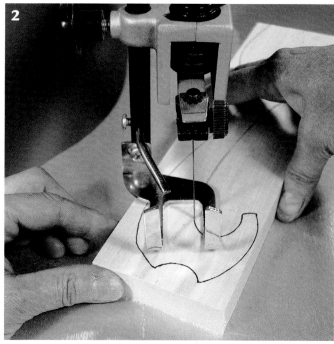

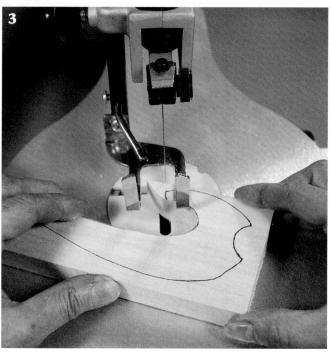

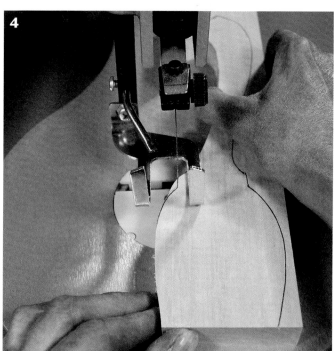

Scroll Saw Rough-Out

During this process we will explore scroll saw work in your wood carving as we create a spoon handle designed to move your stove rack in and out of a hot oven.

1 The scroll saw is a vital power tool that can easily support your wood carving craft. In a few minutes you can rough cut any wooden spoon or cut out a relief carving project, saving you hours of bench knife work.

2 Make a thin cardboard template for your spoon to trace the pattern to your wood. Drop the pressure foot to sit gently against the top surface of your wood.

3–5 With light pressure on the wood, glide the blade along the outside edge of your tracing line. Don't force the wood through the blade cut, allow the scroll saw to do the work. Cut small lengths of the excess wood free as you work. Then readjust the blank to make the next cut.

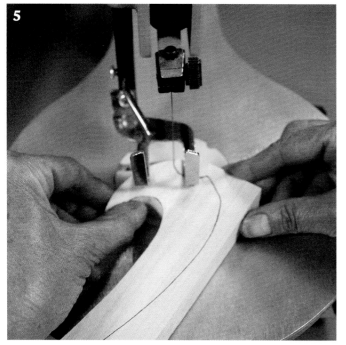

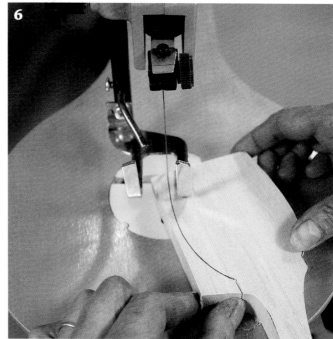

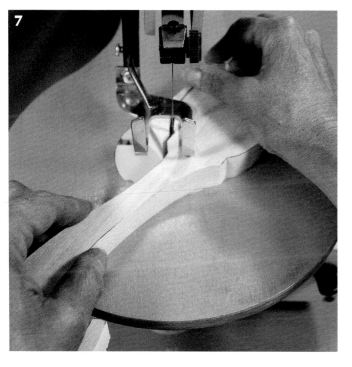

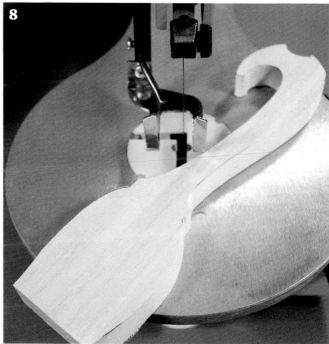

6 As you work any scroll saw project, always know exactly where your hands and fingers are in relation to the cutting blade.

7 Sharp corners and tight curves can be cut in several separate strokes. In photos 6 and 7 the curve of the spoon is cut into the sharp corner. The spoon was then removed from the scroll saw and reset so that the straight side of the corner could be cut, freeing the excess wood along the side of the bowl.

8 A scroll saw rough-cut spoon will have straight, even sides that need only a small amount of shaping and smoothing during the carving steps.

> Always read the manual that comes with your scroll saw. It has full instructions on how to change and tension your blade, and what general maintenance you will need to do.
>
> Follow the safety suggestions in your manual.

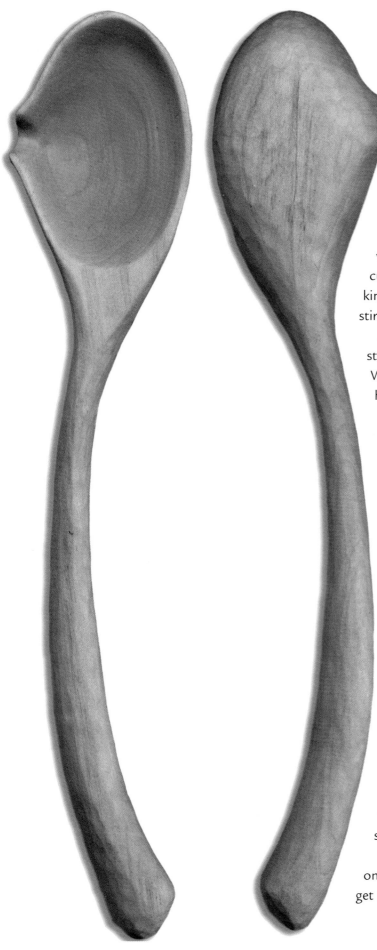

A quick note from one spoon carver to another

Unlike most wood carving projects, spoon carving follows a general method and is not guided by exact measurements.

Spoons are often considered back-porch whittlin's. All our great grandfather needed was a curved-edged pocket knife and a piece of firewood kindling and he was ready to carve a shallow-bowled stirring spoon, flat fork, or pancake spatula.

Straight chisels and round gouges have long been standard tools available to any home woodworker. With the addition of these two basic carving tools he could now work deep bowls, and ladles.

If his kindling was short, he carved short-handled spoons. If the kindling was crocked or bent, he created bent-handled ladles. So it was his tools and materials that determined the final spoon shape, length, and width, not pre-measured patterns.

Throughout the projects in this book we will focus on the general method of spoon carving as how to cut a deep bowl, how to curve the joint between the bowl and handle, and how to decorate your handle.

Also note as you read through any of the projects that I work the entire spoon during each stage of the carving. I do not completely carve, smooth, and sand the spoon bowl and then move into the handle area. Working the rough-out stage through all areas of the spoon, then working the smoothing stage helps me to keep the carving cuts even throughout the work.

By learning the general method to carving a wooden spoon you can create any wood spoon shape or style with any sized piece of carving wood.

So go grab what basswood blocks you have on hand, gather up your carving tool kit, and let's get started!

CHAPTER 4

Projects

Supplies

◈ 12" x 3" x 1" basswood blank
◈ Scroll saw
◈ General cutting scroll saw blades
◈ Safety glasses
◈ Marking pen
◈ Bench knife
◈ Medium round gouge
◈ Wide sweep gouge
◈ Marking pen or #2 pencil for guidelines
◈ 100-, 150-, and 220-grit sandpaper
◈ Crumpled brown paper bag
◈ Clean, lint-free tack cloth
◈ Mineral oil
◈ Large, soft bristle brush
◈ Carving gloves
◈ Large terry-cloth towel

Grandma Shay's
Cookie Dough Spoon

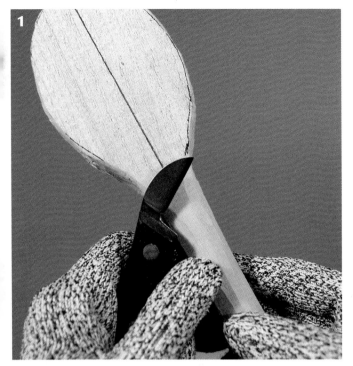

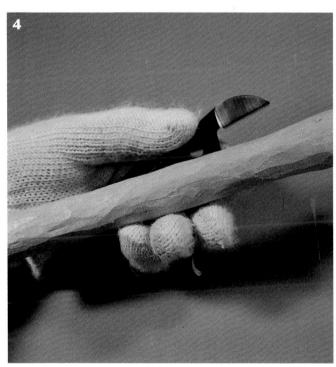

Push-and-pull bench knife strokes

1 With your bench knife, remove any large splinters or rough edges left from the draw knife work. Round over the handle area of the spoon with your bench knife.

2 The bench knife push stroke is worked by placing the cutting edge of the knife at a shallow angle against the wood, and then pushing the knife away from you. The thumb of your holding hand steadies and directs the movement of the blade.

3 The bench knife pull stroke is made with the blade at a shallow angle to the wood and pulling the cutting edge towards you.

4 Use the direction of the wood grain in your handle to determine whether to use a push or pull cutting stroke, always working in the direction of the wood grain.

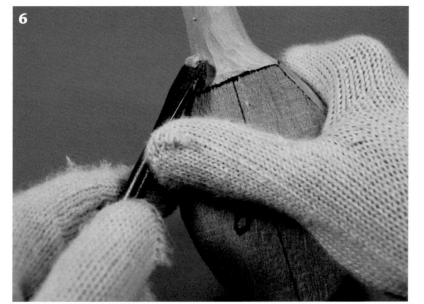

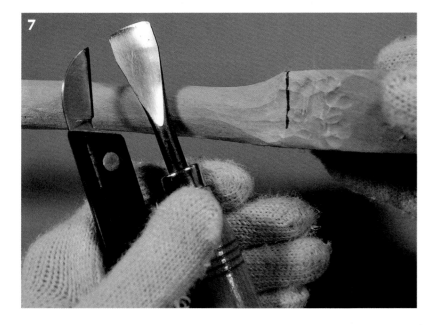

Transitioning the bowl and handle joint

5 Using a marking pen or #2 pencil, mark the back and front of the spoon bowl. In the photo sample, the back of my spoon is noted with the letter "B".

About ⅜" to ½" from the joint of the spoon bowl and handle, mark a straight line across the back and one on each side. This is the area where we will create ears that keep a large, round-bottomed spoon from rolling on the kitchen counter.

6 With your wide sweep gouge, or bench knife, carve the joint area of the spoon back and sides, on the handle side of the joint, below the guidelines just marked.

7 You should have a low, smooth curve that drops the wood from the level of the spoon bowl area into the level of the handle area.

Rounding the bowl back

8 With a marking pen or #2 pencil, mark the back of the spoon bowl to note the direction of the grain of the wood.

   In the photo you can see that the wood grain runs vertically through the spoon. I have marked a horizontal line and vertical line across the center of the bowl. The arrows along the bowl edge show the direction of the knife blade to keep my cutting strokes running with the wood grain.

   I have also marked two lines through the center point of the bowl back on the diagonals. These marks are used to visually guide the roundness of my bowl sides. I can compare the remaining lengths of markings on the bowl to see if I am removing the side wood evenly.

9 Begin rounding over the sides of the spoon bowl by removing the sharp edge left from the draw knife work.

10 Work your push or pull strokes according to the wood grain direction.

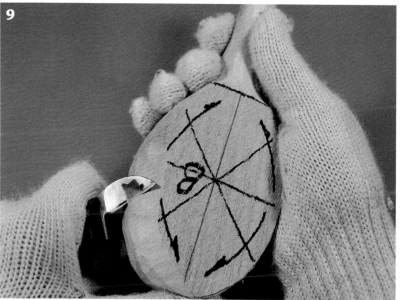

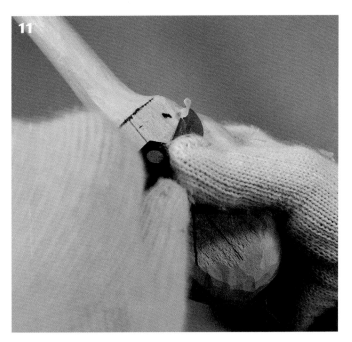

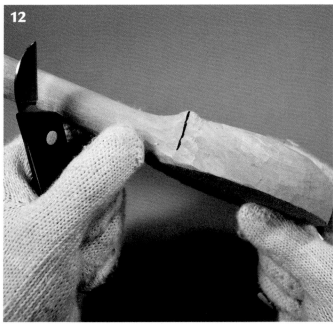

Rounding the bowl back

11 The lower edge of the back of the spoon is where the ears lie. Allow about ½" of unworked, un-carved space above the marked guideline. Cut several push strokes towards the ear area of the spoon handle. Reverse the spoon in your holding hand and work several push strokes to release the first cuts.

12 The worked bowl back is deeply rounded along the front and side edges, and gently tapers into the ear area.

13 How aggressively you round over your bowl back determines how the bowl sits on the kitchen counter top. In this photo the sides are round only on the outer one-third of the bowl back, leaving a flat bottom to the spoon.

Flat-bottomed bowls are excellent for dipping spoons and ladles that can slip their contents if tipped.

14 By taking your rounding cuts to the center of the bowl back you can create a half-circle bowl.

Round-bottom bowls work best for stirring spoons and batter spoons that are glided along the inner sides of a mixing bowl or pan.

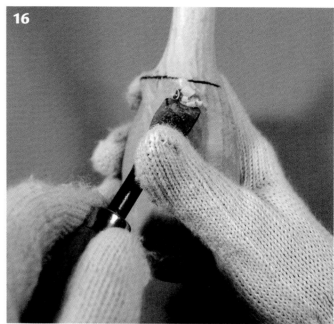

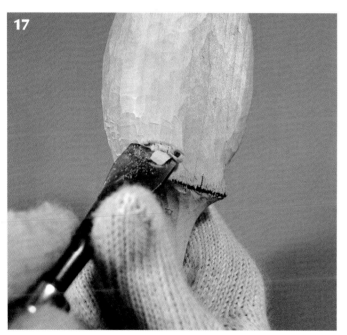

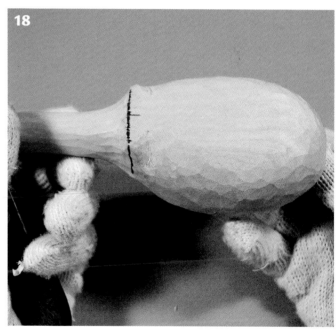

Creating the ears

15 Use a wide sweep round gouge to taper the back center of the bowl into the curvature of the ears.

16 Continue using the wide sweep gouge to deepen the curve on the spoon side of the ears.

17 Make several push strokes into the ear curve area, working from the spoon side of the ears and using the wide sweep gouge. Reverse the spoon in your holding hand and release the push cuts with the wide sweep gouge.

18 At this point in the carving the ear area creates a straight shelf along the full back of the bottom edge of the bowl. Later in this project we will cut out a curved area between the ears to break the shelf into two separate ears. However, you can leave your ear area at this stage. A full ear shelf is a common spoon accent.

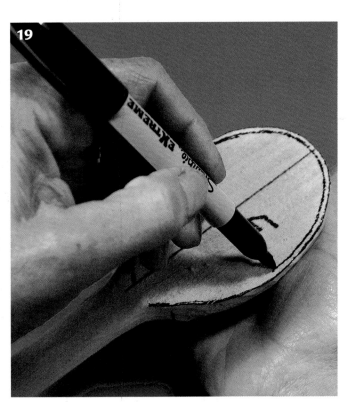

Cutting the bowl

19 With a marking pen or #2 pencil, mark a guideline along the outer edge of the inside or your spoon bowl, allowing about ⅛" thickness from the outer edge of the bowl. This guideline allows you to protect the outer edge of the bowl while you gouge out the bowl's center.

20 With a tight or medium round gouge, begin carving out the bowl of the spoon. Work your cuts from the guideline along the outer edge in to the center of the bowl.

Safety First: Even with carving gloves I always hold my spoon bowl inside of a thick terry-cloth towel during the rounding steps. The towel adds extra protection against a push stroke with a round gouge from slipping out of the bowl and into your holding hand.

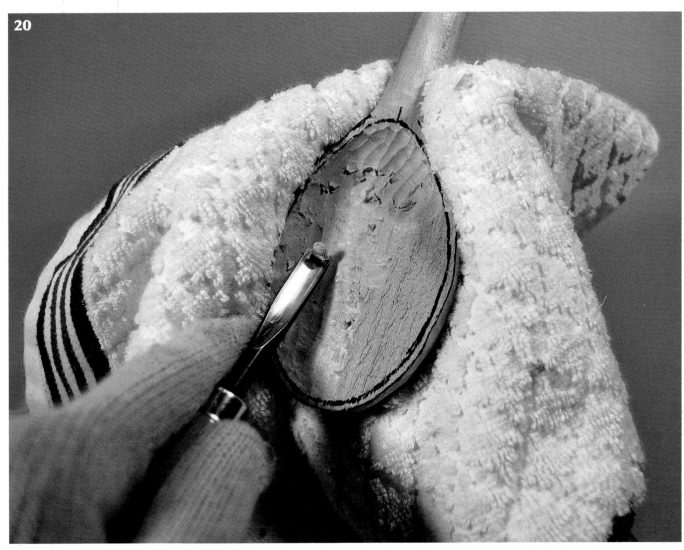

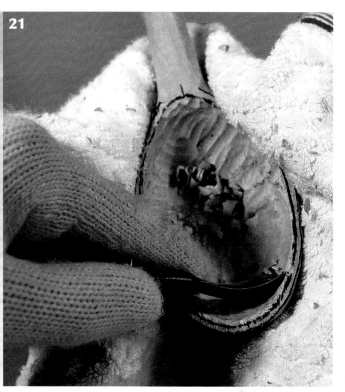

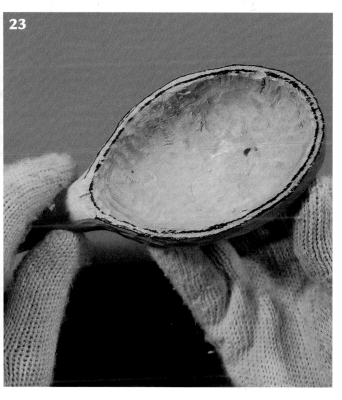

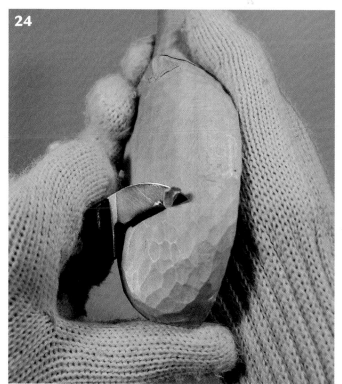

21 A bent round gouge allows you to drop the cutting edge of your gouge deeper into the spoon bowl. Continue your cutting by starting each new push stroke at the edge of the bowl, working towards the center of the bowl.

22 The curve of a bent gouge can be used to lower the center bottom of the bowl.

23 The rough-out of the spoon bowl should have even thickness along the top spoon edge, and taper evenly along the sides to the center bottom.

24 I prefer to leave the bowl slightly thick at this point in the carving. You can use your fingers—one on the outside of the bowl and one on the inside—to gauge the thickness and evenness of the rough-out.

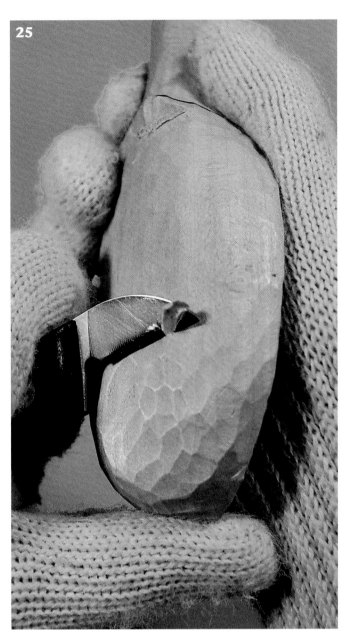

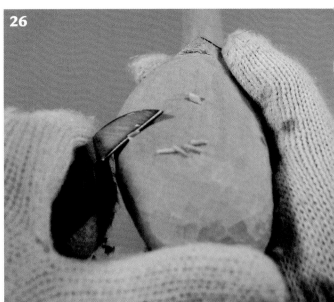

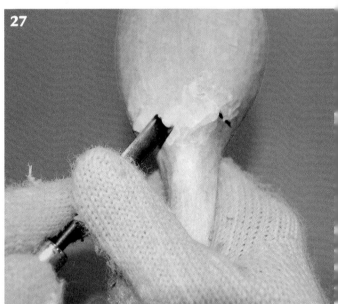

Shaving strokes

25 With the inside of the bowl rough cut, you can use your bench knife to re-carve the back of the bowl to match the curvature of the inside area.

26 Smoothing out the rough-cut strokes is done with a cutting stroke called "shaving." Hold the knife blade low to the wood so that very thin slivers of wood are cut with each stroke.

Work several passes of shaving strokes to create as smooth a surface as possible.

27 With a medium round gouge cut a dip or curve between the ears on the back of the spoon. This separates the ears from one long shelf into two ears, one on each side of the spoon back.

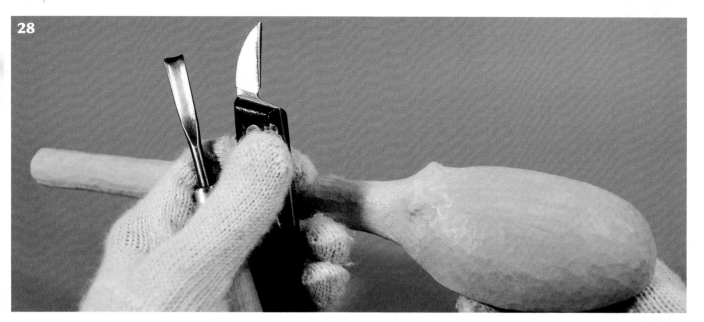

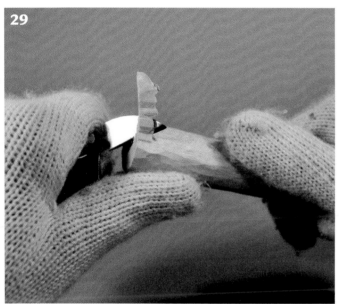

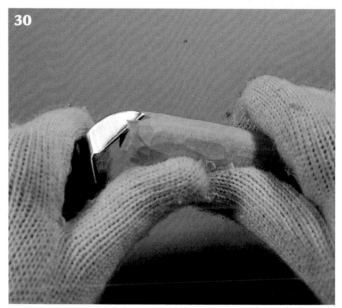

Rounding the handle end

28 The shaved bowl back, the added curve between the ears, and the gentle taper from the bowl to the handle completes the carving work on the spoon back.

29–30 Round over the handle tip using your bench knife.

Shaving with a round gouge

31 The shaving stroke can also be worked using any round gouge by holding the cutting edge low to the wood and gently slicing thin cuts. Shave the inside of your bowl to remove the ridges left from the rough-out stage.

32 With a bench knife, cut a taper along the outer edge of the bowl to round the inside edge into the curve of the bowl. The outer edge is left sharp.

Graduated sanding

33 Your spoon can be left in the shaved stage to allow the texture of your carving cuts to remain as a fine texture to the spoon, or you can use sandpaper to give the spoon a pristine, smooth finish.

34 Use a series of sandpaper, working from 100-, 150-, 220-, to 320-grit, to smooth any remaining cutting ridges or plains. Work the sanding motion with the grain of the wood to avoid creating fine, cross-grain scratches.

35 Tear a 6" square section of brown paper bag and crumble the paper into a ball. Use the ball of brown paper as if it were sand paper. Paper is an extremely fine abrasive and will remove any remaining fibers from your spoon.

Dust well with a clean, dry brush to remove the sanding dust.

Oil finish

36 Brush one generous coat of mineral oil to your spoon. Brush out any thick drips or puddles. Allow the oil to set for about five minutes to soak deeply into the wood.

37 With a dry, lint-free cloth, wipe the excess oil from the spoon. Rub the spoon briskly with the cloth to brighten the shine of the oil.

Several coats of mineral oil may be necessary to give your spoon an even shine. Let each coat dry for several hours before applying the next coat.

Over time and with use, the spoon will naturally lose this oil finish. At any time you can refresh your wooden spoon by applying a new coat.

Mineral oil finish

Wood carving uses many different wood finishes from polyurethane, varnish, spray acrylic sealers, and oil finishes. Most of these finishes are inappropriate for kitchen spoons because they are not food safe.

Mineral oil is food safe and easy to apply. It ensures that any spoon you carve, no matter how decorative in nature, can be used as a cooking utensil.

You do not need to add any finish to your spoon carving. Over time your spoon will pick up a natural layer of finish from the oil, butter, and margarine that you use in your cooking. If you leave your spoon in the raw wood stage you can work the brown paper bag step several times to give it a soft sheen.

And no finish will keep your spoon from developing a natural, dark patina from use. As shown in Grandma Shay's Cookie Spoon, over time it has developed an almost black tone from all the different ingredients with which it has been used.

All of these basic utility spoons are worked using the basic instructions for Grandma Shay's Cookie Dough Spoon. They are rough cut from 8" long, 2½" wide by ¾" deep basswood blanks.

Left to right:
Saucepan Spoon, pattern page 129
Deep Dry Scoop, pattern page 129
Low Curved Scoop, pattern page 131
Scooped Spatula, pattern page 130
Round Melon Spoon, pattern page 131

Supplies

- 12" x 3" x 1" basswood blank
- Scroll saw
- General cutting scroll saw blades
- Safety glasses
- Marking pen
- Bench knife
- Medium round gouge
- Wide sweep gouge
- Marking pen or #2 pencil for guidelines
- 100-, 150-, and 220-grit sandpaper
- Crumpled brown paper bag
- Clean, lint-free tack cloth
- Mineral oil
- Large, soft bristle brush
- Carving gloves
- Large terry-cloth towel

Oven Rack Spoons

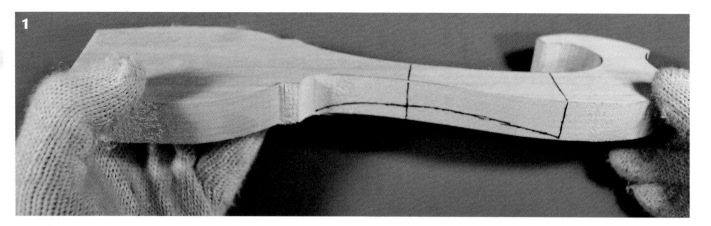

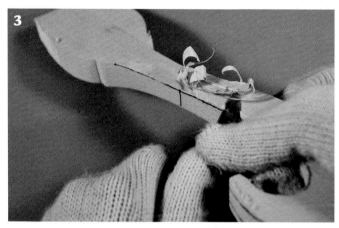

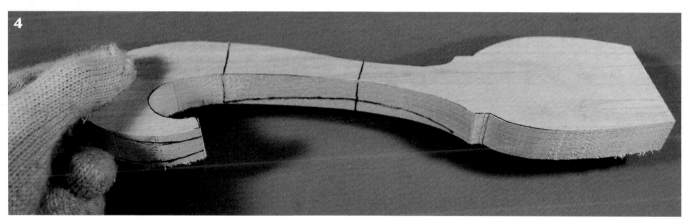

Shaping the handle curve

Once you have used the scroll saw to create a rough cut of the oven rack spoon (see page 18), you can begin to make refinements with your bench knife. The back side of our Oven Rack Spoon handle has a gentle arc or curve.

1 With a marking pen, create a guide line along the sides of the spoon handle from the sharp corner at the back of the bowl to a line parallel with the tip of the oven hook. The curve, at its deepest point, should be one-half the thickness of the handle about 1¼" from the sharp corner of the bowl.

2–3 Using the bench knife, cut the marked curved area in the back side of the handle to bring the handle thickness down to match the guidelines on both sides.

4 This gentle back-side curve drops the bowl area of the spoon slightly below the level of your holding hand.

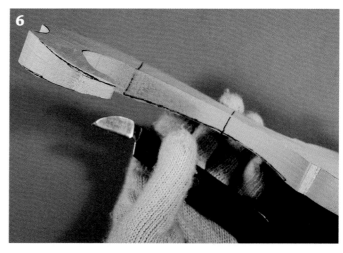

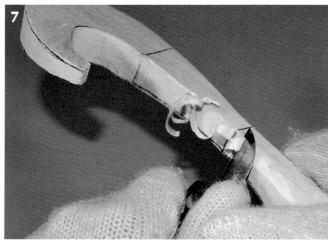

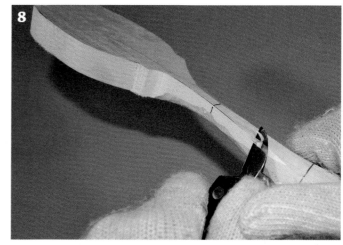

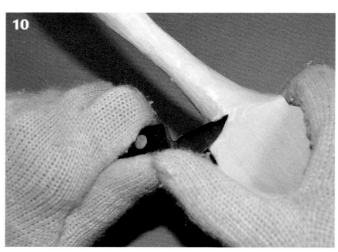

Rounding the handle

5–6 Using the bench knife, taper the end of the handle hook to ¼" thickness at the hook point. Work the tapering on both the front and back of the handle area.

7–9 Begin rounding over the sides of the handle to remove the harsh square edges left from the scroll saw cutting.

10 Taper the bowl and handle joint on the back of the spoon, working from the square corners at the end of the bowl into the handle curve.

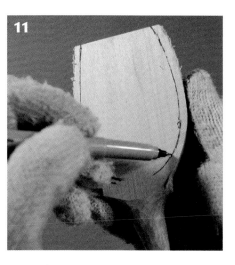
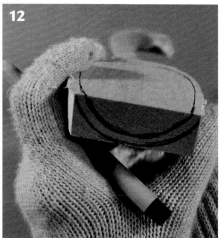
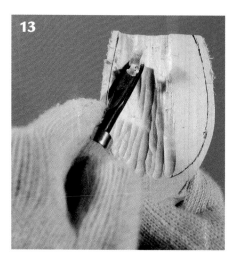

Carving the inner bowl

11–12 With a marking pen, create a guideline along the top side of the bowl about ⅛" from the cut edge. Create two guidelines for the curve of the front edge of the bowl, allowing ⅛" between the two lines.

13 Our oven rack spoon has a classic scoop shape at the front of the bowl. Use your medium or large round gouges to rough out the inside of the bowl area. Allow the gouge cuts to remove all of the wood at the front of the bowl to create the scoop opening.

14 The completed scoop bowl is tightly arced at the handle side of the bowl, dropping quickly to the floor of the bowl. The floor then has a slight, gentle slope to the scoop opening.

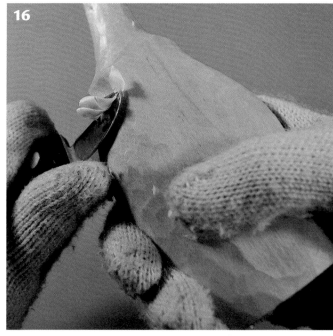

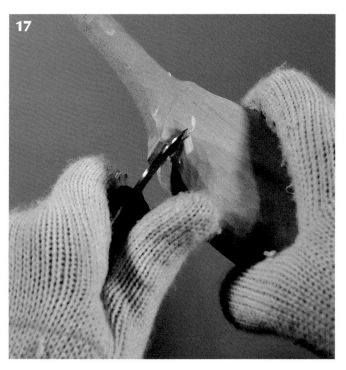

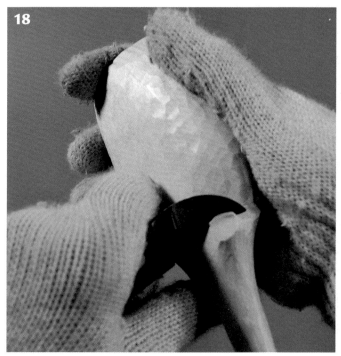

Shaping the bowl back

15 Using your bench knife, round over the back side of the bowl to match the curvature of the inside scoop shape.

16 Round the bowl into the square corner handle joint.

17-18 Using your bench knife, cut a straight line along the bowl and corner joint to create a crisp joint line.

This scoop has a flattened back at the center of the bowl area that keeps the spoon from rolling on the counter. Only the sides of the bowl back are worked in the shaping steps.

The curvature of the back of a spoon bowl does not need to mirror the inner curve of the bowl. In this project the inner bowl needs a deep, tight curve to act as a dry ingredient scoop. But the back of the bowl needs to be flat so that the scoop does not tip over when filled with flour.

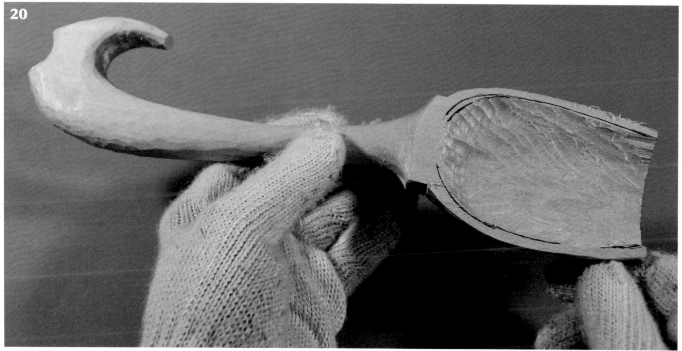

Rough-cutting steps completed

19-20 In these photos you can see the completed rough-cutting stage of carving. Our oven rack spoon has a very round center to the handle that gradually flattens as the handle reaches the oven hook edge. The inner front bowl has a very tight and deep curve, with a flat central back area.

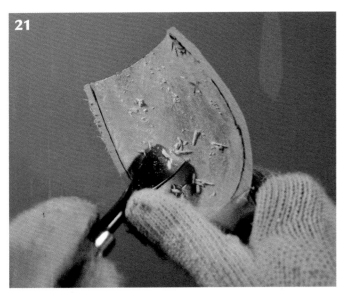

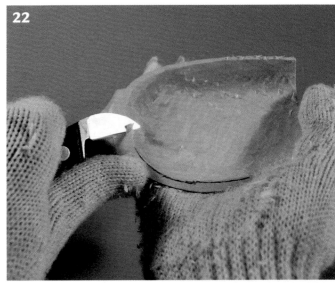

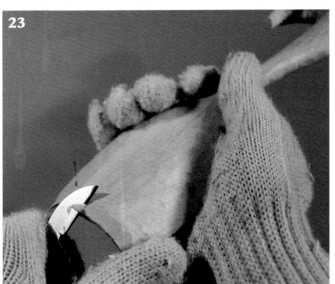

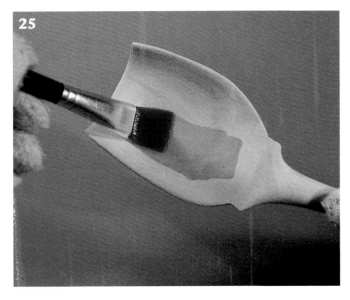

Shaping and shaving the bowl

21 Using a wide sweep gouge or bent gouge, shave the front inner bowl area to a smooth, even curve.

22 With your bench knife, gently roll over the edge along the inside of the bowl.

23 Taper the back front edge of your scoop with the bench knife.

Mineral oil finish

24 Smooth the entire spoon using a graduation of sandpaper grits from 150- through 320-grit.

25 Dust the spoon well with a dry, lint-free cloth. Apply one to two coats of mineral oil. Allow the oil to penetrate the wood for about five minutes, and then wipe off any excess oil.

Spoons can have either straight, gently curved, or deeply curved handles.

Left to right:
Saucepan Spoon, pattern page 129
Right-Handed Spatula, pattern page 134
Left-Handed Saucepan Spoon, pattern page 134
Hook Handle Spoon, pattern page 133
Small Oven Rack Spoon, pattern page 127

Supplies

- 8" x 2" x 1" basswood blank
- Bench knife
- Medium or large bent round gouge
- Medium or large straight round gouge
- Wide sweep gouge
- Small round gouge
- Marking pen or #2 pencil for guidelines
- 100-, 150-, and 220-grit sandpaper
- Crumpled brown paper bag
- Clean, lint-free tack cloth
- Mineral oil
- Large, soft bristle brush
- Carving gloves
- Large terry-cloth towel

Tasting Spoons

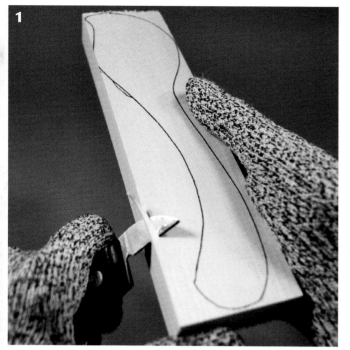

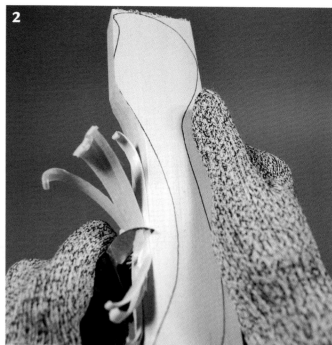

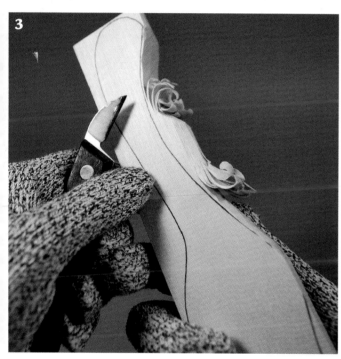

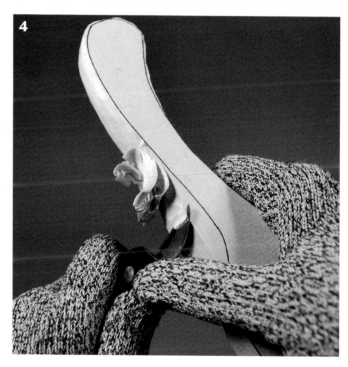

Rough cutting the general spoon shape

1 The bench knife can be used to cut the general shape of your spoon. Work the cutting edge of the knife with the direction of the wood grain of your basswood blank as much as possible.

2 Take thin slivers of wood with each cut by keeping the blade angle low to the wood. Taking too deep a cut at the beginning of the stroke can cause your knife to bind up as it goes deeper into the wood. If this happens, simply back the knife out of the deep cut and re-cut along the sliver taking a shallower, thin approach.

3–4 Curves can be cut by first creating a series of push cuts towards the center point of the curve. Reverse the spoon blank in your hand and make a second series of push cuts to release the first.

Work along the sides of the template patterns to free the spoon shape from the blank.

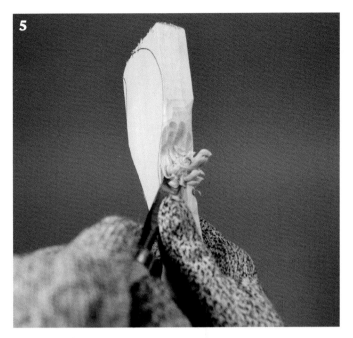

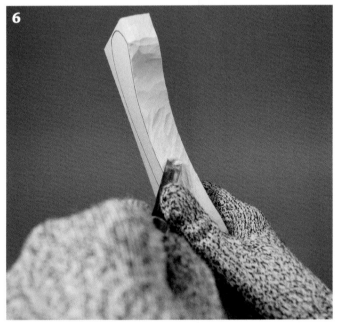

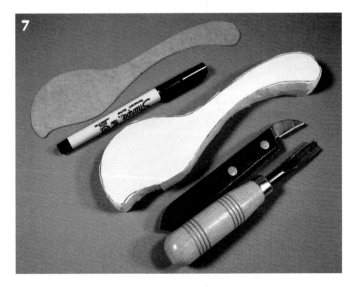

Gouge cutting tight curves

5–6 Tight curves can be worked in shaping your spoon using a small or medium round gouge. You can cut a series of push strokes with the gouge, working towards the center point of the curve. Reverse the blank in your hand and work the other side of the curve, freeing the first push strokes.

Smooth out the gouge cuts by holding the round gouge at a very low angle to the wood and making diagonal cuts across the curve area. This shaves the high ridges left from the gouge rough out.

7 For this tasting spoon I have added a small curved point on the front edge of the spoon bowl. The point is perfect to reaching into the corner at the bottom of any mixing bowl where the flour tends to pile up under the wet ingredients.

You can add a small mixing point to any spoon design and that little change will quickly make your hand-carved wooden spoon the cook's favorite.

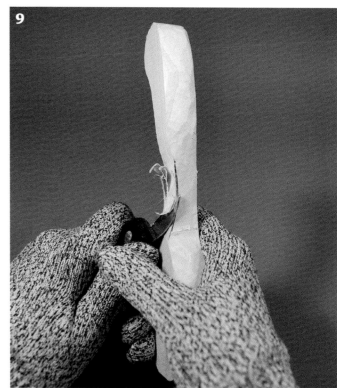

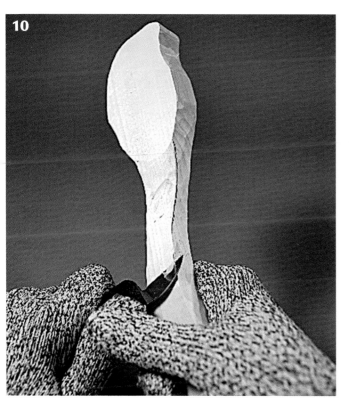

Marking the guidelines

8 Using a marking pen, mark a curve from the bottom end of the bowl to about one-half the length of the handle on both sides of the spoon. This area on the back of the handle will be removed to give a gentle curve to the handle area.

Shaping the handle curve

9–11 Use either the bench knife or a medium round gouge to reduce the wood on the back in the marked curve area. Taper the level change from the bowl into the curve area with a tight-arced drop. The taper of the curve on the handle side is a long, slow drop.

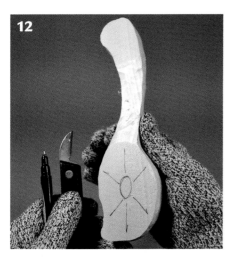

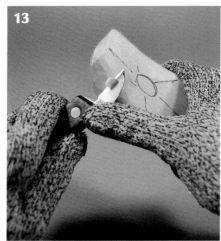

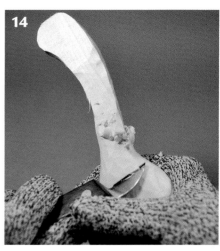

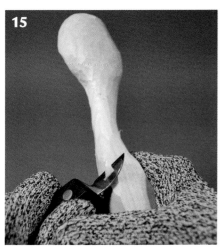

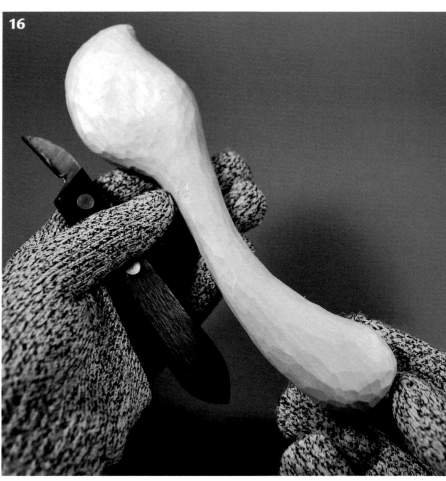

Rounding the spoon back

12–13 With a marking pen, create your back bowl guidelines to establish the direction of the bench knife cuts around the bowl's edge. For this spoon, I left the center bowl back flat so that the spoon will not roll on the counter. The small guideline oval, shown in photos 13 and 14, notes where the flat area will lie. A second flat area is left in the center of the handle tip bulb.

14–15 Round over the edges of the spoon handle back. Gently blend the bottom end of the bowl back into the handle area using your bench knife.

16 The general shaping of the spoon's back is complete. You can see the two flat areas—one in the bowl's center and one in the center of the handle bulb. This design has a very rounded back profile in contrast to its flat-front face.

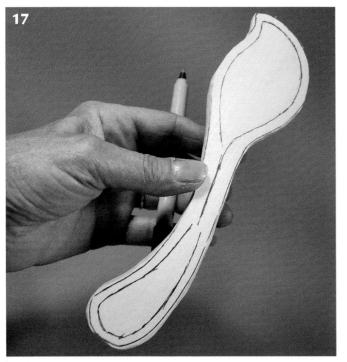

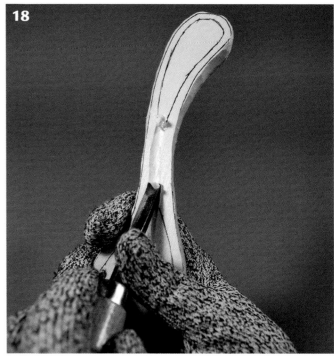

Cutting the tasting bowls

17 Mark a guideline for the large bowl on the front of the spoon. Make this line fall ¼" from the edge and bring the side guidelines to a point where the bowl meets the handle area. Create a second guideline for the smaller tasting bowl area on the spoon handle. Mark this line ¼" from the edge of the cutout. Join the two bowl area guidelines with a straight line down the center of the handle.

18–20 Working with a small, medium, and bent round gouge, begin cutting the shape of both tasting bowl areas. Join the two areas with a cut along the straight guide line that is one gouge-width wide.

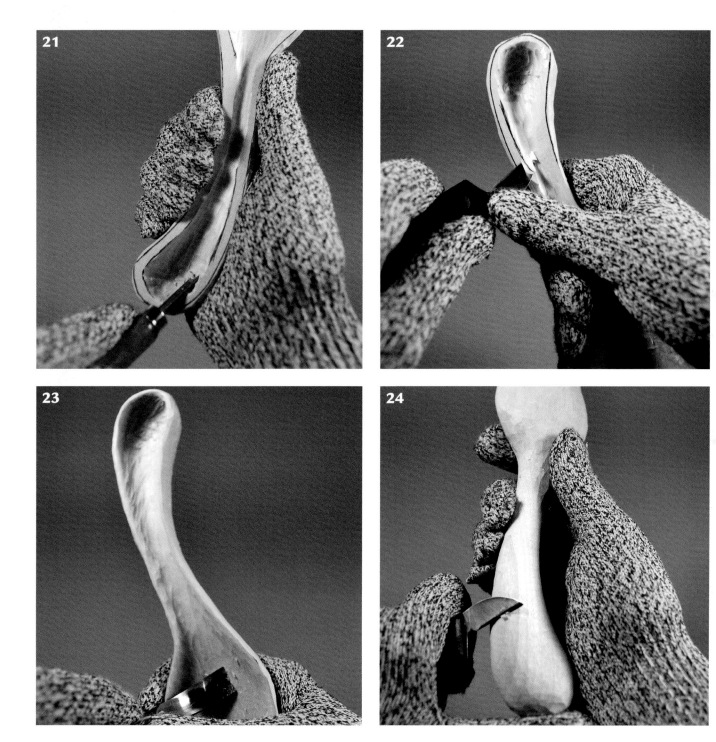

Shaving the bowl areas

21–23 Use your round gouges at a low angle to the wood to shave the inside of both bowl areas into a smooth finish. Round over the inner top edge of the bowl areas using your bench knife.

24 Using your bench knife, lightly shave the entire spoon to remove any remaining rough-cut ridges.

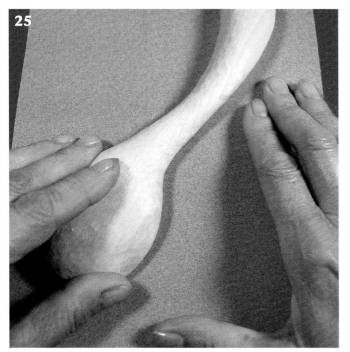

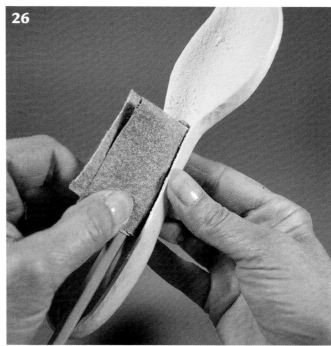

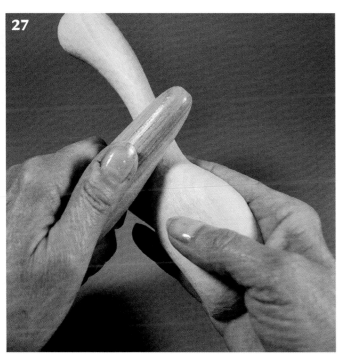

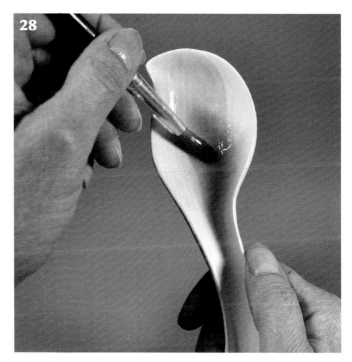

Sanding

25 To ensure that the front edge or front face of the spoon is perfectly flat, lay the spoon face down onto a sheet of 150- to 220-grit sandpaper. Rub the spoon across the paper until the entire face has been worked. Repeat this step using 320-grit sandpaper.

26 The inside of the trough between the stirring bowl and the tasting bowl can be sanded by wrapping your sandpaper around a pencil, brush handle, or a small round-handled carving tool.

27 If you wish to leave this spoon in the raw wood stage, burnish the wood to a bright sheen by rubbing it briskly with a carving tool handle. The rubbing process presses any remaining fibers tightly into the wood.

28 If you prefer an oil finish, apply one to two coats of mineral oil and allow the oil to soak in for about five minutes. Wipe any excess oil with a clean, dry, lint-free cloth.

Supplies

- 13½" x 3" x 1" basswood
- Scroll saw
- General cutting scroll saw blades
- Safety glasses
- Bench knife
- Medium or large bent round gouge
- Medium or large straight round gouge
- Wide sweep gouge
- Marking pen or #2 pencil for guidelines
- 100-, 150-, and 220-grit sandpaper
- Crumpled brown paper bag
- Clean, lint-free tack cloth
- Mineral oil
- Large, soft bristle brush
- Carving gloves
- Large terry-cloth towel

Modern Texture Spoons

Texture can play an important part in your spoon carving, adding both visual impact and a better gripping surface for your cook. Textured areas and smooth finishes have been mixed and matched in the four small Leaf Spoons above.

Left to right:
The inward scroll turned-handle spoon uses texture on the handle with a smoothed, sanded inner bowl area. The top curl handle spoon was carefully sanded to a completely smooth finish over the entire spoon. The outward scroll handle spoon was worked with texture for the entire spoon, then three fine v-gouge lines were cut into the handle area. The double scroll handle spoon was worked with a heavy, rough textured effect.

Scroll Leaf Spoons, pattern page 141

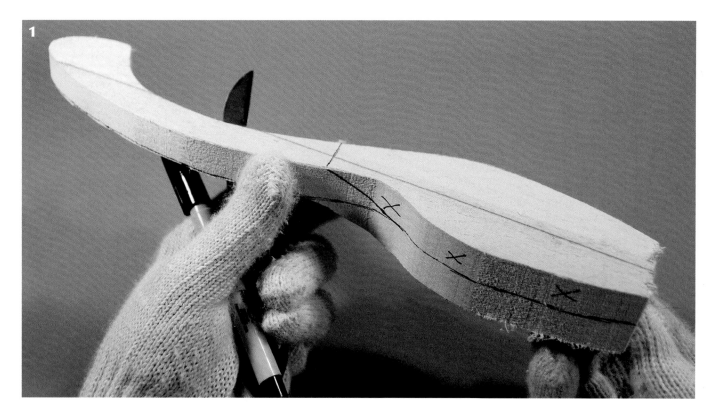

Modern Texture Bacon Fork

Bacon forks usually have a bent handle joint between the handle and fork tines to drop the front edge of the fork comfortably against the frying pan bottom. The tines are wide with a large split between them to lift and drain the bacon strip.

1 Begin by tracing your pattern to the wood blank. Use your bench knife, scroll saw, or coping saw to rough cut the spoon shape from the blank. I cut my blank using the scroll saw.

With a marking pen, make a guideline along the sides of the fork bowl at one-half the thickness of the wood blank. At the handle and bowl joint, mark your guideline on the side to slope up to the top surface of the blank. Mark small x's in the top one-half of the thickness of the bowl. This will be the area that we will remove to create the handle bend.

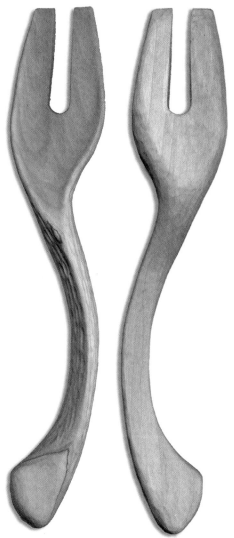

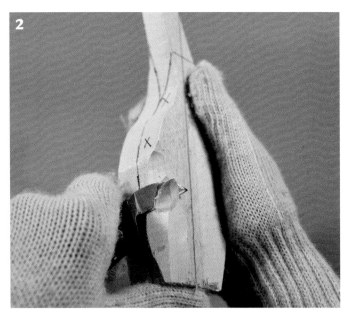

Reducing the bowl area

2 Begin removing the top one-half of the bowl wood by rutting along the outer edge with the bench knife. Bring the cuts down to the guidelines on the side of the spoon.

3 Use a wide sweep gouge to remove the wood in the central area of the fork bowl.

4 Note in the photo that the fork bowl slowly and gently slopes from the handle area to the front of the fork edge.

Taper the front edge of the fork

5 Create a second guideline along the sides of the fork bowl that tapers from the center point of the fork bowl to the front edge, dropping the front edge width by one-half.

6 Use your wide sweep gouge to re-cut the bowl area to thin the front half of the bowl down to the new guideline.

7 The rough cut of the fork bowl shows the gentle taper from the original surface level at the handle down to one-half thickness at the center of the fork bowl, and again to one-quarter of the original thickness to the front edge of the fork.

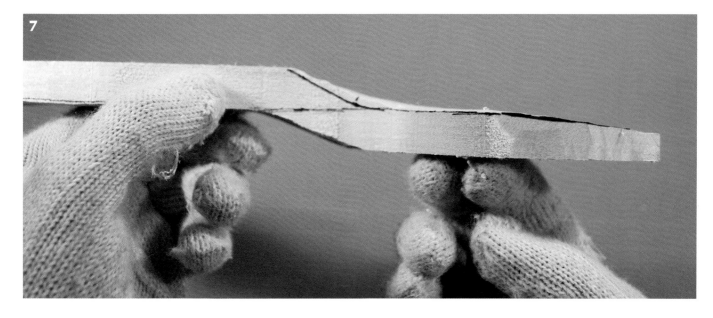

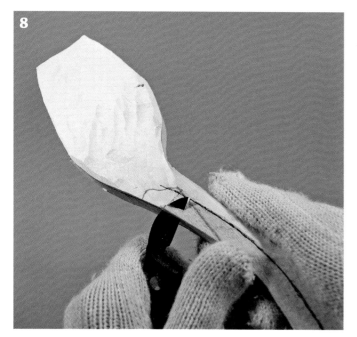

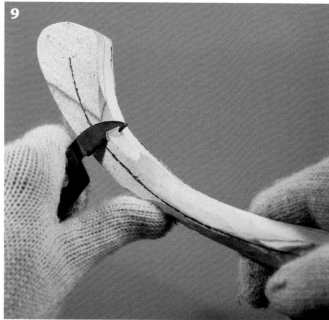

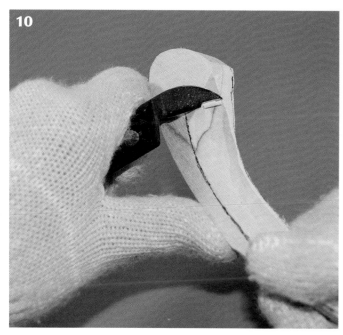

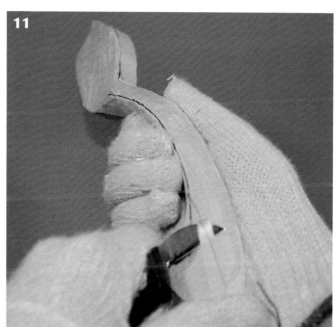

Creating the triangle shape of the handle

8 With a marking pen, create a guideline on the top of the handle that runs down the central line of the handle. The triangle shape will be worked from this guideline.

9 Slope the top sides of the handle area, working your cuts from the center guideline to the bottom edge of the sides. The guideline becomes one sharp edge of the triangle shape, with the two sloped sides and the fork back becoming the three flat sides of the triangle.

10–11 Continue the triangle shape of the handle up to 1" from the handle end.

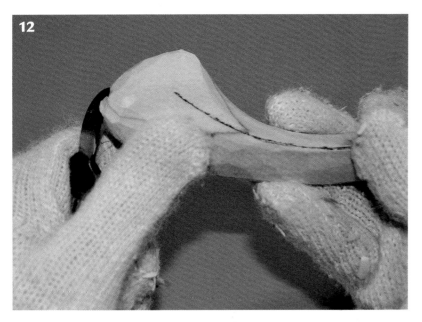

12 Leave the last 1" of the handle flat, or un-carved on the handle tip. Round over just the edges of this area, using a bench knife.

13 Round over the sharp edges of the triangle areas of the handle, removing any remaining guideline marks.

14 With a marking pen, create a guideline for the fork shape along the edge of the fork bowl, marking the line about ⅛" from the edge.

Note in the guideline that the fork bowl extends to a round point into the handle area.

Use your medium or small round gouge to begin the shaping of the bowl area. Taper the bowl, shaping from the handle area the deepest curves of the fork bowl at the handle joint.

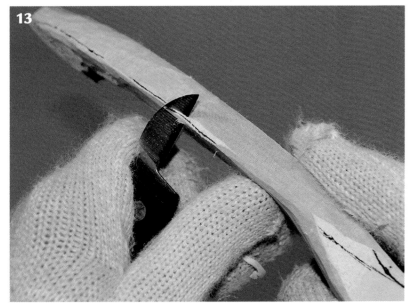

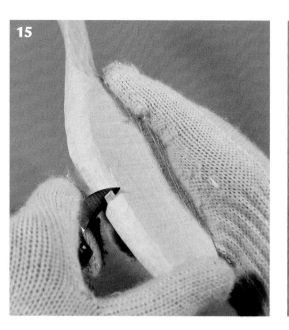

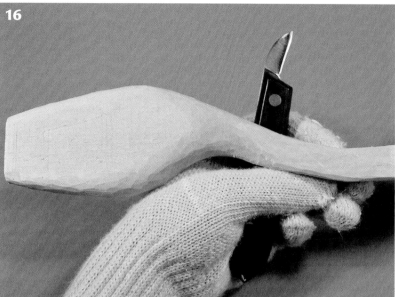

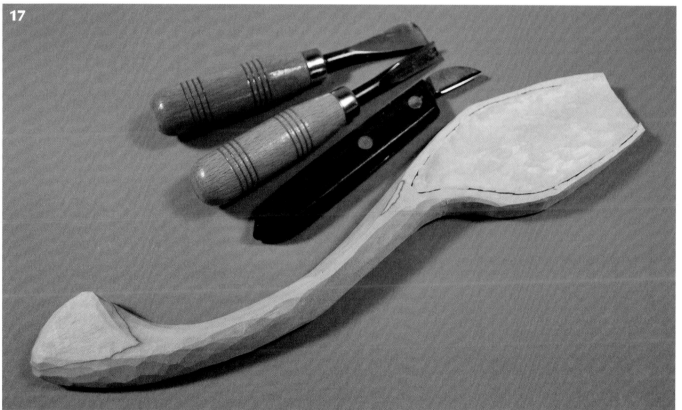

Rounding the edges on the back

15 Use your bench knife to round over the back side edges of your fork bowl. Leave the front back edge of the fork bowl with a sharp lower edge.

16–17 The completed rough-cut work will give the fork a flattened back that has a straight line into the back of the fork bowl. The front side of the fork has a triangular point down the center of the handle and then drops to one-half the thickness of the handle into the fork bowl.

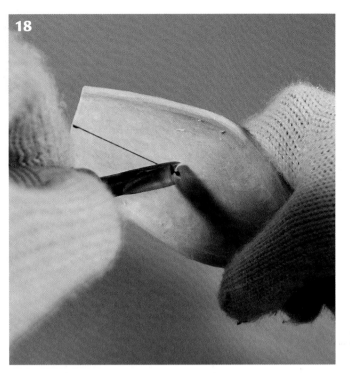

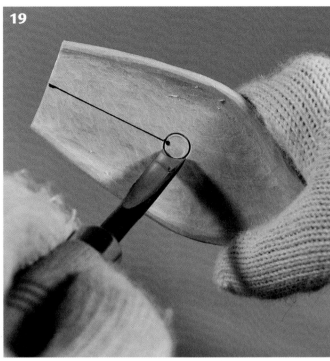

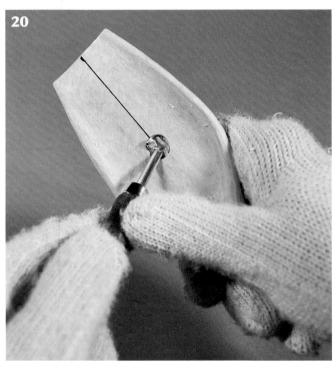

Cutting the fork tine slot

18–19 Mark a 2½" long guideline in the center of the fork from the front edge towards the bowl back. This is the center line of the fork slot. Up-end a medium round gouge and center the cutting edge at the end of the guideline. Roll the gouge in your fingers, gently pressing the cutting edge into the wood. The rolling motion will cut a perfect small circle that matches the arc of your gouge blade.

20–21 Use a small round gouge to carve out the small up-end cut of the medium round gouge. Repeat these two steps—up-ending the medium gouge followed by removing the cut circle with the small round gouge—until you have carved the hole completely through the fork. Use your bench knife to clean up any small chips or fibers.

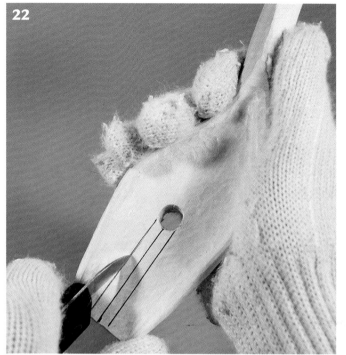

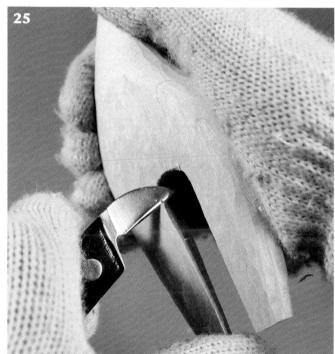

Cutting the slot

22 Mark two guidelines, one on each side of your up-ended hole from the hole to the edge of the fork. Cut along the guidelines with your bench knife, keeping the knife in an upright position.

23–24 Angle the tip of your bench knife slightly and cut a second line from the center of the slot into the first straight cut line. Repeat several times until you have cut through the guideline on both sides of the slot.

25 Use your bench knife to clean up and trim the inside edge of the fork slot.

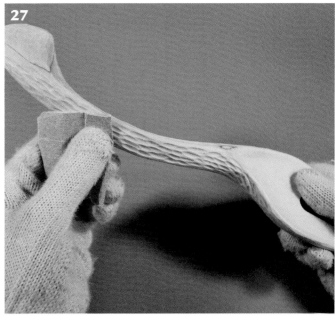

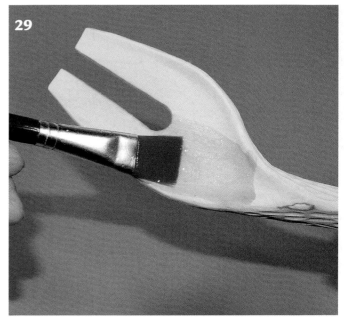

Cutting the texture

26 The texture on the handle of our Modern Textured Bacon Fork is created using small cuts worked in the direction of the wood grain with a small round gouge. This lifts a small, shallow trough cut. Work the gouge cuts so that one cut overlaps another to layer the handle with texture.

27 Lightly sand your bacon fork using a graduation of grits from 150- to 320-grit sandpaper.

28 Roll a small section of the sandpaper around a pencil, ¼" wooden dowel rod, or small carving tool handle to sand the inside edges of the slot.

29 Remove any sanding dust with a dry, lint-free cloth. Apply one to two coats of mineral oil to your fork. Allow each coat to soak into the wood for about five minutes. Wipe the excess oil with a cloth.

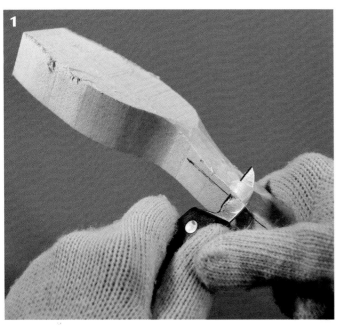

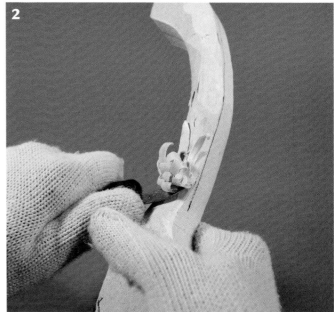

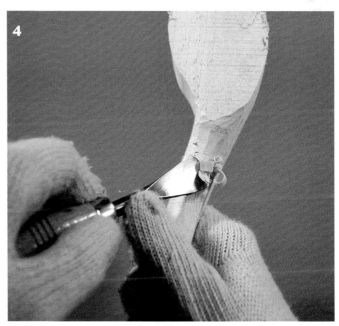

Modern Texture Ladle

Our Modern Texture Ladle, shown on page 136, follows the same steps as the Modern Textured Bacon Fork. The only changes in this project are in the creation of the ladle bowl and spout, and that only the handle area is reduced because the ladle bowl needs all of the thickness of the wood blank to create a deep bowl.

1 Trace your pattern to the wood blank and cut out the blank to free the spoon shape. For my modern texture ladle I used my scroll saw. Mark a guideline with a marking pen, one-half the thickness of the wood, through the handle area of the spoon on both sides of the spoon.

2–3 Using your bench knife, carve away the excess thickness in the handle on the back side of the spoon, from the back edge of the bowl area to about 1"–1 ½" from the bulb tip on the handle. Taper this central handle slope at both the end of the bowl shape and the bulb handle area.

4 Working on the front of the spoon, begin working the triangular cutting for the handle, tapering the joint between the bowl and the handle. See steps 8–13 for the Modern Texture Bacon Fork, pages 57–58.

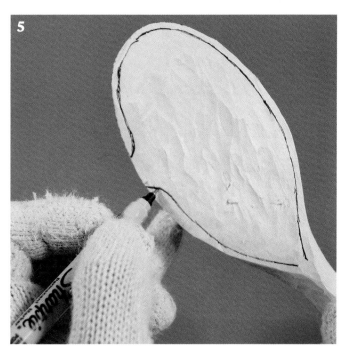

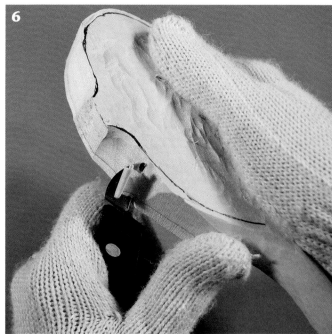

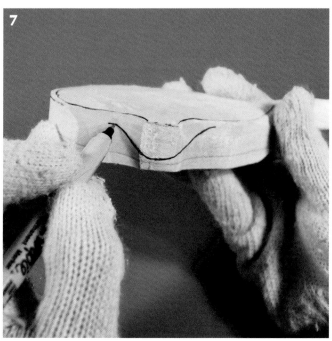

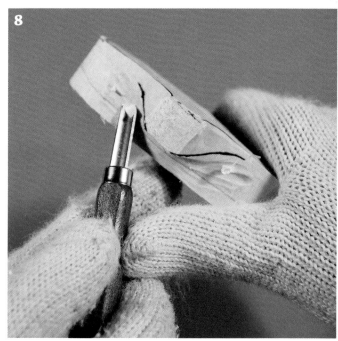

Shaping the ladle bowl

5 The general cut-out shape of the ladle begins with the same shape as any stirring spoon. With a marking pen, create guidelines around the bowl's edge about ⅛" from the edge of the wood. At the center point on one side of the bowl, bring the guidelines out to touch the edge of the wood, with a ⅜" to ½" space between the lines. This will be the ladle spout.

6 With your bench knife, carve along the side of the ladle bowl on either side of the spout to allow the spout to extend beyond the sides of the ladle bowl.

7 With a marking pen, create a guideline to note the bottom edge of the spout area on the side of the ladle bowl. The lowest point of the ladle spout stops about ⅛" to ³⁄₁₆" from the bottom edge of the overall ladle bowl.

8 With a small or medium round gouge, carve the ladle bowl area to drop the bowl behind the ladle spout. The spout extends about ¼" to ⅜" beyond the side of the ladle bowl.

Rounding the back of the ladle bowl

9 With a marking pen, create guidelines on the back of your ladle bowl to note the center of the bowl and the wood grain direction.

10 With your bench knife, begin rounding over the back edges of the ladle bowl. Work the entire ladle back to create as round a shape as possible.

11 Shave the ladle back with a wide sweep gouge by holding the gouge at a low angle to the wood to cut very thin slivers with each stroke. Remove any remaining ridges left from the rounding process.

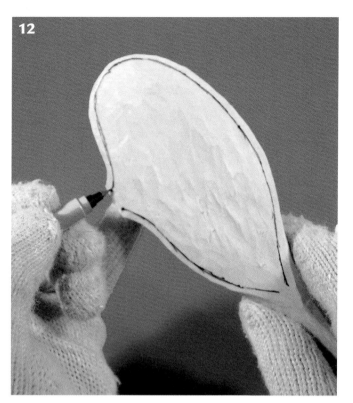

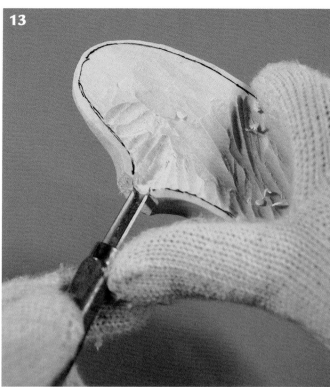

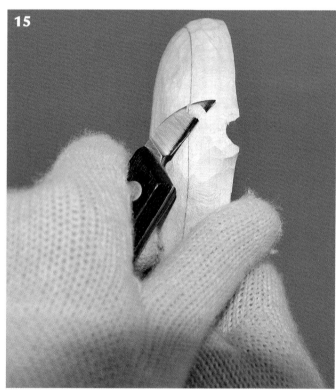

Shaping the inside of the ladle bowl

12 Re-mark your guideline for the inside shape of the ladle bowl, if necessary.

13 Using a small round gouge, cut the opening of the ladle spout. The depth of this area is about one-half the total depth of the ladle bowl.

14 Using a medium or bent round gouge, shape the inside of the ladle bowl. Shave the bowl with a wide sweep gouge.

15 Smooth the outer portion of the ladle spout using your bench knife.

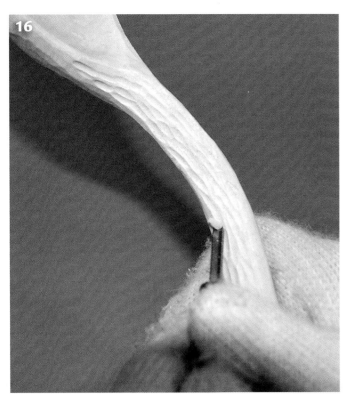

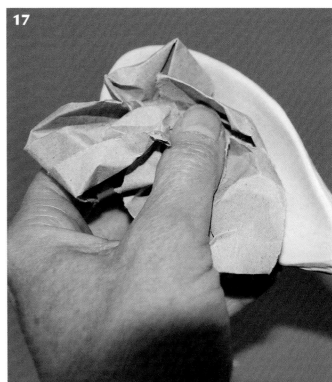

Adding the texture and oil finish

16 Using a small round gouge, create the texture cuts along the handle area of the ladle. Hold the gouge at a low angle to the wood and cut short strokes, allowing the strokes to overlap.

17 With a graduation of sandpaper grits, from 150- to 320-grit, lightly sand the handle of the ladle. Sand the inside of the ladle to a smooth finish. Complete your sanding step using a piece of a crumpled brown paper bag.

18 Apply one to two coats of mineral oil to the entire ladle with a soft bristle brush. Allow each coat to absorb into the wood for about five minutes, then remove any excess oil with a dry, lint-free cloth.

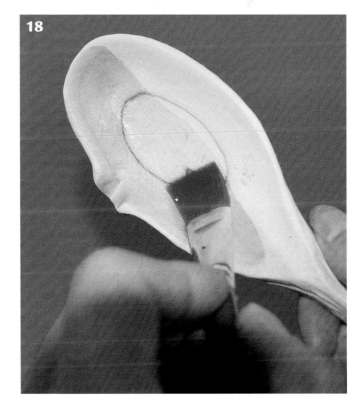

Supplies

- 12" x 3" x ½" basswood blank
- Scroll saw
- General cutting scroll saw blades
- Safety glasses
- Bench knife
- Medium or large bent round gouge
- Medium or large straight round gouge
- Wide sweep gouge
- Marking pen or #2 pencil for guidelines
- 100-, 150-, and 220-grit sandpaper
- Crumpled brown paper bag
- Clean, lint-free tack cloth
- Mineral oil
- Large, soft bristle brush
- Carving gloves
- Large terry-cloth towel

Simple Thin Spoons

Because salad forks and spoons are designed to lift, flip, and toss, they do not need to have the deep bowls or thick handles of stirring spoons. That thinness allows us as carvers to exaggerate the handle, bowl, and tine shapes of our wooden spoons.

In this project we will work through the basic steps to create a salad spoon and fork.

1 Begin by tracing your pattern to the wood blank. Cut out the basic shape of the spoon using a scroll saw, coping saw, or bench knife. Thin, ½" stock wood is often too thin to easily work with a draw knife. Both of my samples were cut with the scroll saw.

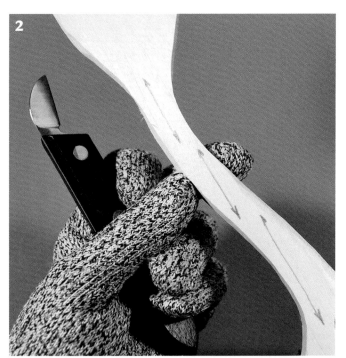

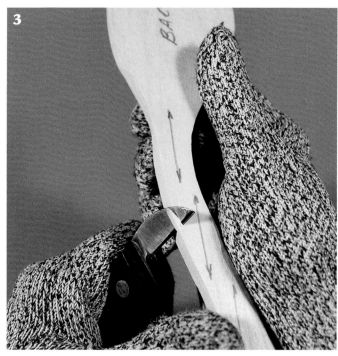

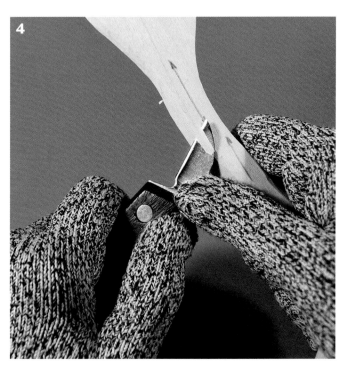

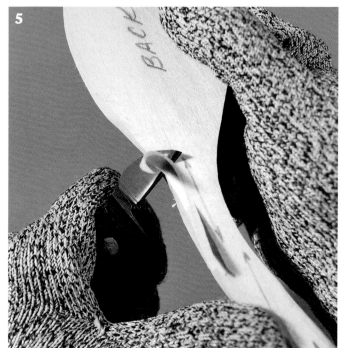

Working with the wood grain direction

2–5 Because my stock is only ½" thin, it is important to mark the wood grain direction to guide my knife strokes. With thinner stock it is easy to accidentally dig the knife blade in, cutting too thick a stroke, if you work against the grain.

Use your bench knife and the push and pull strokes to round over the edges of the handle areas of your spoon.

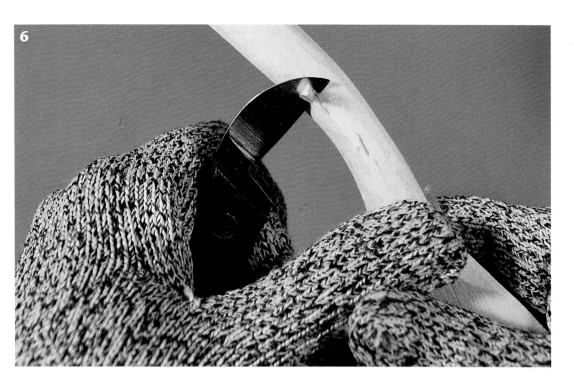

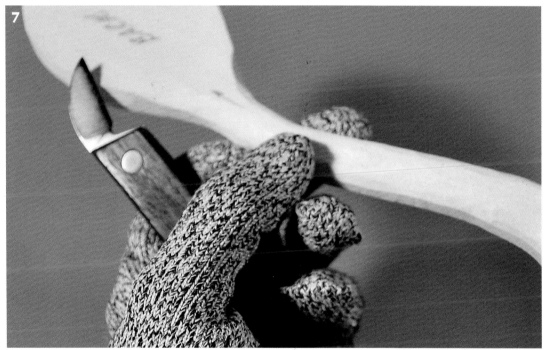

Round the sides of the handle

6 Lay your bench knife blade low to the wood and shave off any sharp or deep ridges.

7 The finished handle will have a flattened look along the top and bottom of the handle, with the sides rounded evenly.

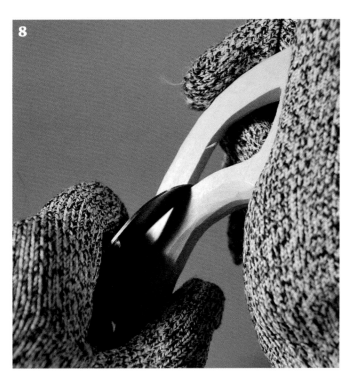

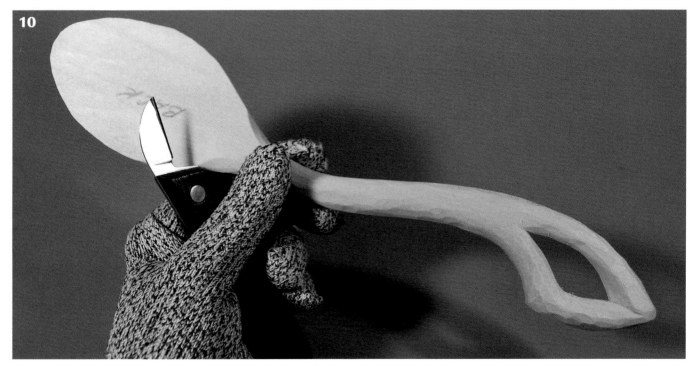

Cutting the handle opening

8 With your bench knife, cut a slice straight into the wood at each point of the handle opening.

9–10 Round over the sides of the handle opening, working the strokes into the slice made in step 8. This will free the cuts as well as round over the sides of the inner points.

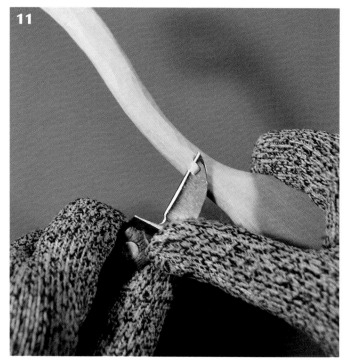

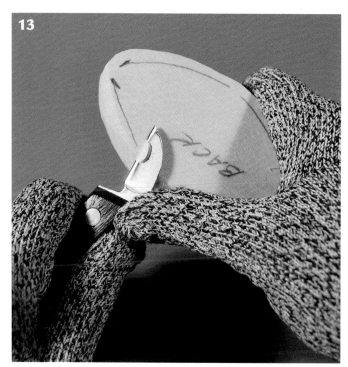

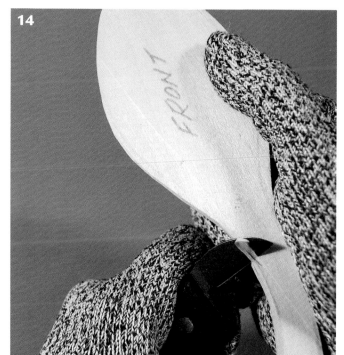

Round over the bowl back

11 Lay your bench knife blade low to the wood and lightly shave the handle and handle opening to create a smooth finish. Taper the back edge of the bowl back into the handle area.

12 Mark your guidelines for the direction of the wood on the back of the spoon bowl.

13 With your bench knife, round over the outer edges of the spoon bowl back. Work the rounding over cuts

about ½" from the sides of the bowl back, allowing the central area of the bowl back to remain at the flat surface of the wood blank.

14 Turn your spoon over to work the front of the spoon. Using a bench knife, taper the back of the spoon bowl front into the handle area.

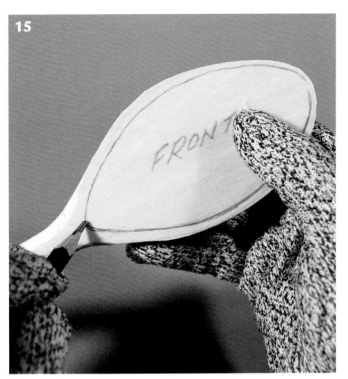

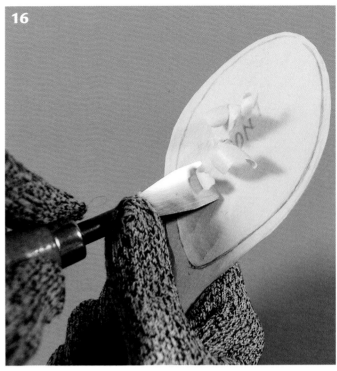

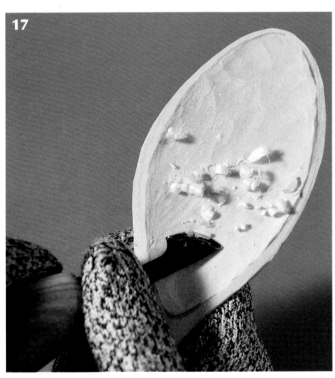

Working the bowl front

15 Using a pencil or marking pen, mark your guideline for the bowl interior about ⅛" from the outer edge of the spoon. For this spoon the bowl shape is a deep oval or tear-drop design.

16 Use a wide sweep gouge to shape the inside of the spoon bowl. You only need to drop the bowl interior about ⅛" to create the bowl shape.

17 With a skew knife, hook knife, or large wide sweep gouge, shave the inside of the bowl to remove any gouge ridges.

18 Use a graduation of sandpapers, from 150- to 320-grit, to remove any remaining cutting stroke ridges. Remove any sanding dust with a dry, clean cloth.

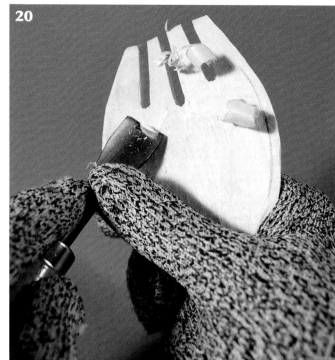

Shaping the fork

19 Because I cut my spoon and fork blank with the scroll saw, my fork tines are already cut. If you are cutting your spoon or fork blank using a coping saw or bench knife, up-end a round gouge, as described in steps 18–25, pages 60–61, for the Modern Texture Bacon Fork.

20–21 Mark a guideline along the outer edge of the fork bowl, about ⅛" from the bowl edge. Using a wide sweep gouge, round down the upper portion of the fork bowl shape. Taper the bowl to about ⅛" thick at the tine end of the bowl.

Sanding and oil finish

22 Sand your fork through a graduation of sanding paper grits, from 150- to 320-grit. Remove any sanding dust with a dry, clean cloth. Do a final polishing of your salad set with a crumpled brown paper bag.

23 Apply one to two coats of mineral oil to your fork and spoon. Allow each coat to absorb into the wood for about five minutes, and then remove any excess oil with a dry, clean cloth.

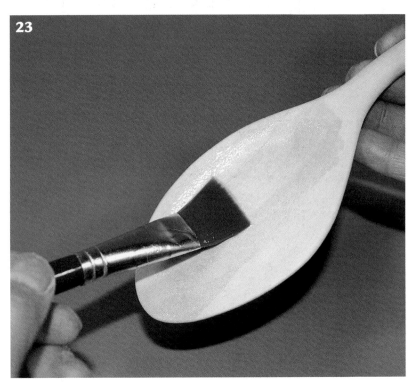

Pyrography Spoon Set

Thin-stocked wooden spoons are excellent for your next pyrography project. This set, which includes a spoon, slotted spoon, and fork, were worked following the same steps as our Thin Wood Salad set.

The slots in the slotted spoon were cut by up-ending a medium round gouge as shown in steps 18–21, Modern Textured Spoons.

The henna flower pattern was traced to the spoons after the sanding steps were completed and then burned using a variable-temperature pyrography unit and a ball-tip pen. The set is finished with mineral oil.

Supplies

- 12" x 3" x ½" basswood
- Scroll saw
- General cutting scroll saw blades
- Safety glasses
- Bench knife
- Large chip-carving knife
- Medium or large bent round gouge
- Medium or large straight round gouge
- Wide sweep gouge
- Marking pen or #2 pencil for guidelines
- 100-, 150-, and 220-grit sandpaper
- Crumpled brown paper bag
- Clean, lint-free tack cloth
- Mineral oil
- Large, soft bristle brush
- Carving gloves
- Large terry-cloth towel

Chip-Carved Spoons

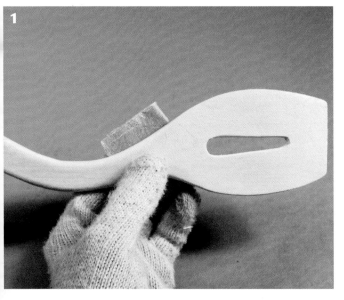

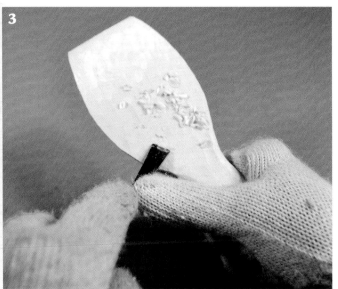

In this project we will combine the general shape patterns from the Modern Textured Spoons with the thin-wood stock carving of the Thin Wood Spoons and add a chip-carved decoration to the handles. Chip carving is a technique which creates small, deeply set triangles into the wood. Those triangles can be combined to create intriguing arrangements.

Once you have learned the basic skills of spoon carving, it is exciting to mix and match patterns, techniques, and design accents to create new styles of spoons.

Chip-Carved Spoon Patterns: The chip-carved spoons use the same general shape cutting patterns as the Modern Texture Spoons shown on page 52-67.

Carving the slotted spoon

This project uses the same general shaping steps as the Thin Wood Spoons in the previous project. Take a few moments and read through that project before you begin the work on this Chip-Carved Salad Set.

1 Trace your pattern to thin-stock basswood. Cut out the general shape of your spoon with a scroll saw, coping saw, or bench knife.

2–3 Follow steps 19–21 for the Thin Wood Salad Fork to thin and taper the bowl area of the slotted spoon. The front edge of the spoon should taper to about 1⁄8" thick at the front edge.

4 Lightly sand the spoon to a smooth finish using a graduation of sandpaper grits, from 150- to 320-grit. Remove the sanding dust with a dry, clean cloth.

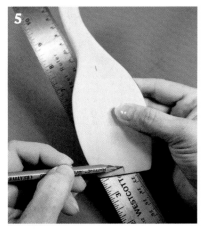

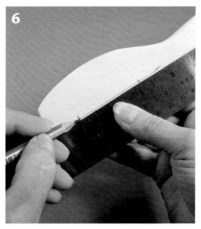

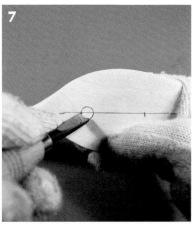

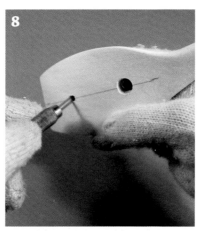

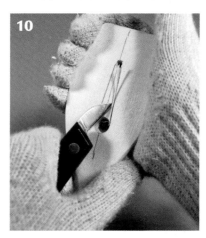

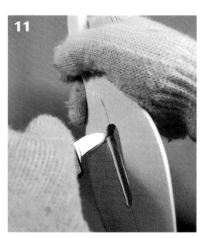

Cutting a slotted spoon

5 With a ruler and pencil, mark the center line of the slotted spoon bowl.

6 Measure ½" from the front edge of the spoon and make a mark. Measure 2½" from the front edge and make a second mark. Draw a straight line between these two marks, this is where your slot will fall inside of the spoon bowl.

7 Up-end a medium round gouge at the 2½" mark, centering the gouge to the guide line. Roll the gouge to cut free a medium-sized hole.

8 Up-end a small round gouge at the ½" mark. Roll the gouge to cut free a small hole.

9 With a ruler and pencil, draw a line on each side of the holes, to connect the two cut holes. These lines are the side lines of the slot.

10 With your bench knife, cut along the two side slot guidelines just made to free the wood inside of the slot.

11 With your bench knife, trim the sides and holes of the slots smooth.

12 Fold a sheet of medium-grit sandpaper (150- or 220-grit). Slide the sandpaper into the slot hole and sand along the sides. Work a second sanding using 320-grit sandpaper.

Sand the full slotted spoon with graduations of sandpaper grits, from 150- to 320-grit. Remove any sanding dust using a dry, clean cloth.

Cutting a serrated pie knife

13 Using a scroll saw, coping saw, or your bench knife, cut the general shape of this serrated knife from your wood blank. Follow the general shaping directions for the Thin Wood Fork, shown in steps 19–21 on page 75.

14 Taper the thin edge of the knife bowl towards the side edge of the knife blade to about ⅛" thick.

15 With a ruler, mark a line ¼" from the knife blade edge as a guideline for your serrations.

16 Measure and mark every ¼" along this guideline. This will establish the distance between each serration.

17 With a pencil, create a diagonal line from the edge to the ¼" marks on the guideline to create the v-shaped spaces of the serration points.

18 With your bench knife, cut from the outer edge of the knife along one of the diagonal lines to the ¼" guideline.

19 Working from the other edge towards the ¼" guideline, cut the second diagonal line of the v-shaped serration.

20 Repeat cutting free the v-shapes between the serrations of your blade. You can use any size of measurement between your serrations to create very fine, shallow v-shapes, to very heavy, open v's.

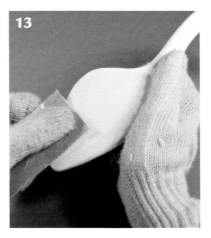
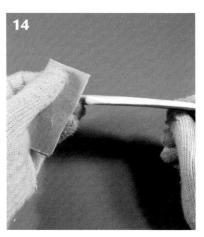
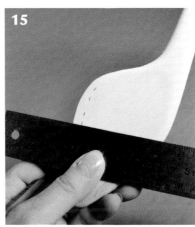

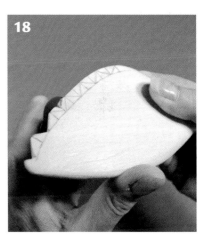
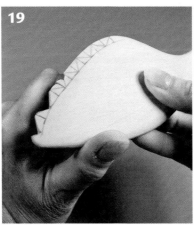
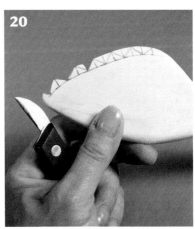

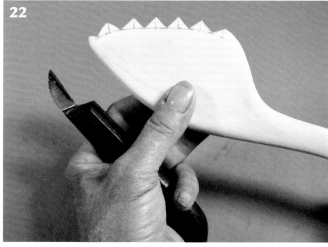

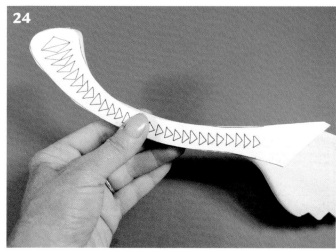

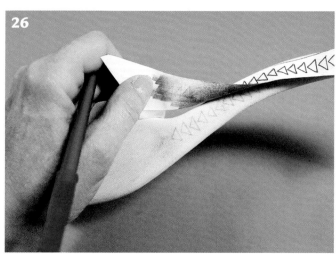

Finishing the serration cuts

21–23 Complete the cutting of your serration v's. With a graduation of sandpapers, from 250- to 320-grit, smooth the entire surface of the pie knife, slotted spoon, fork, or spoons before you begin the chip-carving process. Remove any sanding dust with a dry cloth.

Tracing the chip-carving pattern

24–26 Make a copy of the chip-carving handle pattern onto computer paper. Cut the pattern section free from the paper. Rub the back of the pattern with a soft, #4 to #6, pencil. Lay the pattern over the handle area and tape into place using transparent tape. With an ink pen, trace the pattern to your spoon handle.

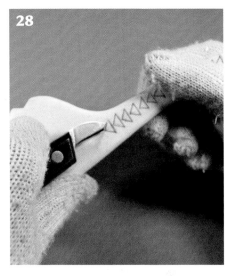

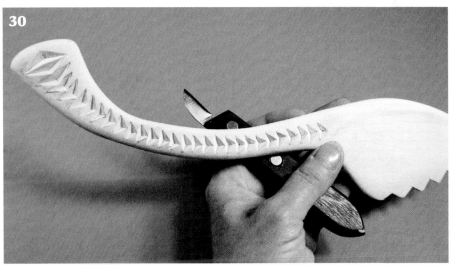
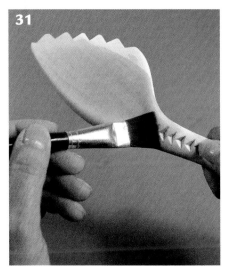

Cutting a chip

27 The basic chip-carved triangle is a three-stroke process using the large chip-carving knife. Each cut of the three strokes is angled or pointed towards the central bottom point of the triangle area.

Start your first cut along one outer point on one side of the triangle. Lay the knife at a 22 to 25 degree angle to the wood. Pull the knife tip along the pattern line, slowly deepening the tip into the wood at the center of the line. As you finish the cut of this line, slowly bring the knife tip back out of the wood.

28 Turn your spoon to work the second straight line of the triangle. Repeat the same cut and angle as the first stroke.

29 Turn your spoon to work the final, third line of the triangle. Repeat the same cut and angle as used with the first two strokes. The third stroke frees a small triangle chip from the wood.

30 Repeating steps 27–29, cut each of the chip triangles in the traced design.

31 With 320-grit sandpaper, lightly sand the chip-carved handle to remove any remaining tracing lines.

Remove any sanding dust with a dry, clean cloth. Apply one to two coats of mineral oil with a soft bristle brush. Allow each coat to soak into the wood for five minutes, then wipe off any excess oil with a dry cloth.

> As a general habit, I do a test cutting for any chip-carved pattern onto scrap basswood before I begin the cutting on my project. On page 110 you can see a practice board sample cut for one of the Wedding Spoon patterns.

Supplies

- 12–14" x 2½" x 1¼" basswood
- Draw knife
- Non-skid kitchen mat
- Clamps
- Bench knife
- Large chip-carving knife
- Medium or large bent round gouge
- Medium or large straight round gouge
- Wide sweep gouge
- V-gouge
- Marking pen or #2 pencil for guidelines
- 100-, 150-, and 220-grit sandpaper
- Crumpled brown paper bag
- Clean, lint-free tack cloth
- Mineral oil
- Large, soft bristle brush
- Carving gloves
- Large terry-cloth towel
- Painter's or masking tape

Rustic Twist Handles

With just a few strips of painter's tape and your variety of widths of round gouges, you can add wonderful twists to any spoon pattern handle.

Cutting the general spoon shape

1 Begin this project by tracing your pattern to the basswood blank. Use a draw knife to cut the general spoon shape from the blank.

With your bench knife, round over the entire handle area of the spoon. The handle, at this stage of the carving, is about 1" in diameter, which allows extra room to cut the twist pattern.

2 Use the bench knife to gently taper the back end of the spoon bowl into the handle joint.

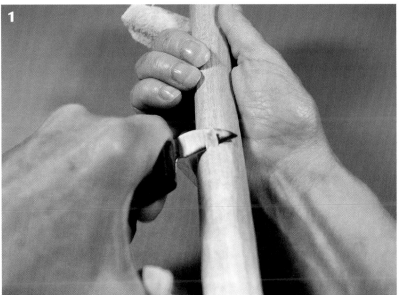

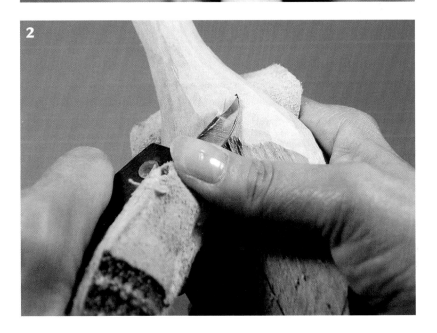

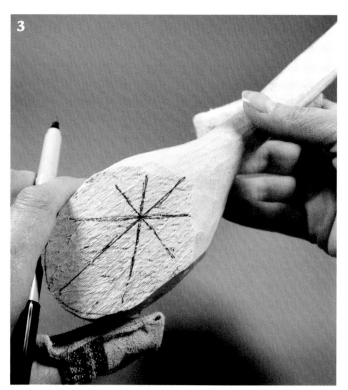

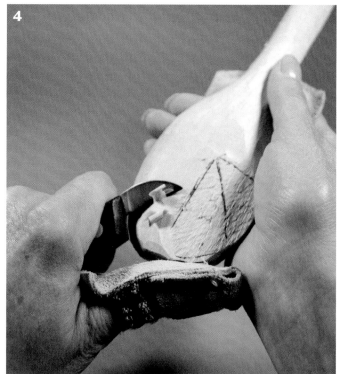

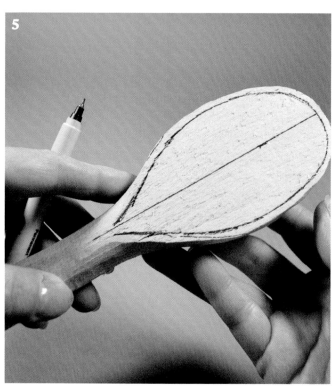

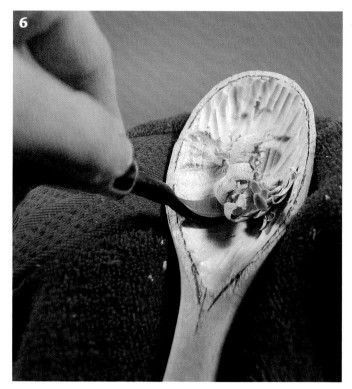

Shaping the spoon bowl

3–4 With a marking pen, mark the back of your bowl with the wood grain guidelines to establish the center point of the bowl back. Use your bench knife to carve away the sides of the bowl back, creating a very round profile with no flat spot at the center.

5–6 Mark your cutting guideline along the outer edge of the front of the spoon bowl, about ⅛" from the wood edge. Use your medium round gouge, bent round gouge, and wide sweep gouge to cut the inside of the bowl.

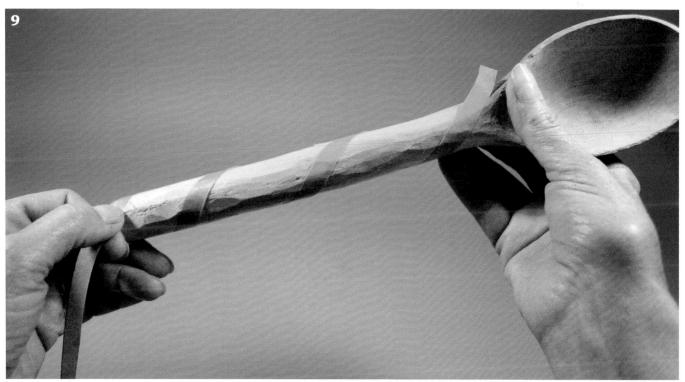

Establishing the twist pattern on the handle

7 Use your wide sweep gouge, hook gouge, or skew gouge to smooth the inside of the bowl. This is not the final smoothing for the bowl area, so you can leave it slightly textured.

8 Cut three strips of painter's tape ¼" wide by about 24" long.

9 Place one strip of painter's tape on the front of the spoon at the bowl and handle joint at a 45-degree angle to the handle. Gently turn the spoon in your hand, wrapping the tape evenly along the full length of the handle. Press into position.

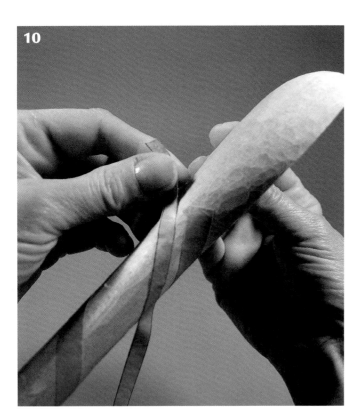

Adding the second and third tape strip

10–12 Repeat steps 8 and 9 with two more strips of ¼" wide painters tape, spacing each new strip of tape about ¼" from the last piece of tape. The three pieces of tape have wide spacing, about ½" to ¾" between each round of the twists. Press each new strip of tape firmly against the wood.

You can easily vary the twist pattern by cutting your tape strips into different widths, from ½" to ⅛" and by varying the distance between the strips.

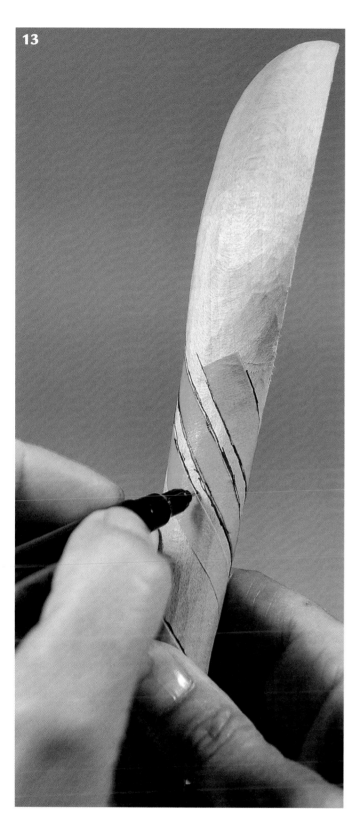

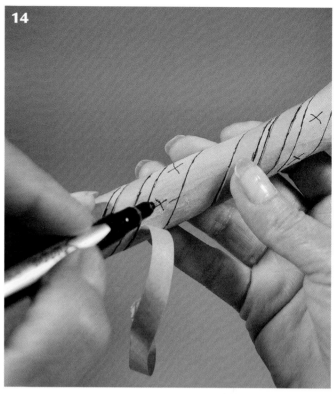

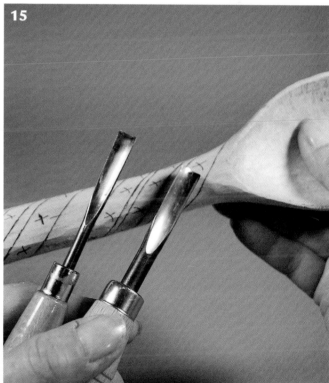

Mark the twist guidelines

13 Use a marking pen to create a guideline along the outer edge of each piece of tape.

14 Remove the tape strips, one at a time, adding a small mark inside of the tape strip area to note where you will be cutting the round trough.

15 As you create the tape twist pattern you can adjust the width and placement of your tape strips to match the width of your round gouge carving tools. In this photo the ¼" thickness of the tape matches one of my medium, straight round gouge profiles.

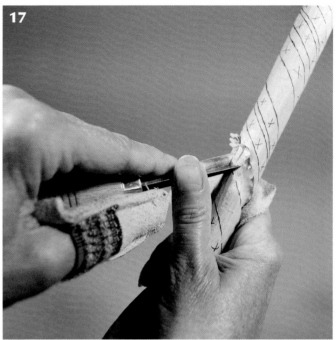

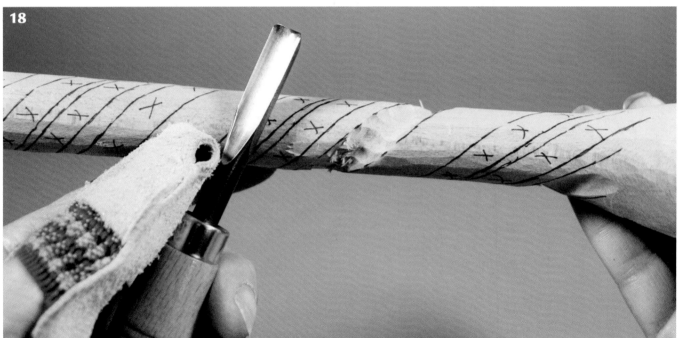

Rough cutting the gouge trough of the twist

16–18 There are two methods to rough-cutting the gouge twist troughs, both of which depend on the wood grain and grain hardness of the handle.

If your handle is a straight, even grain that is easy to cut, you can simply drop the cutting edge of your round gouge between the lines and slowly follow the guidelines in your cutting stroke. One side of the cut will be worked with the grain while the opposite side will be cut against the grain. When you have worked one set of cutting strokes, turn the spoon handle over to re-cut the trough, working the second side with the wood grain.

If you are using a hard wood or a wood blank that has erratic wood grain patterns, you can rough-cut the trough by working small gouge chips from the top guideline towards the center of the trough. Then reverse your spoon handle to cut the second side of the trough, again working from the outer guideline towards the center of the trough area.

Safety first

19 Working a round gouge across the rounded surface of the spoon handle cause the gouge to slip out of the cutting stroke, creating a dangerous situation and possible injury. For that reason I always wrap my twisted spoon handles in several layers of thick terry-cloth towel in my holding hand.

The towel will not prevent the gouge from slipping out of the cut, but it does minimize the possibilities of injury.

Working the second and third twist

20–21 Using your round gouge, rough-cut the second and third twist lines. Note in step 21 that a small un-carved space is left between each twist trough.

Note in steps 20 and 21 how the beginning of each trough is on the back side of the spoon bowl and is gradually tapered deeper as it is cut into the handle area.

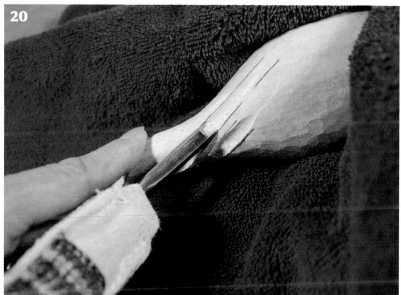

Varying the depth of the twist troughs

22 I chose to re-cut my first twist trough using a slightly wider round gouge. The second and third trough use the same, smaller gouge. You can also vary the depth of one trough from another by re-cutting just one of the twist lines. Both of these techniques make it easy for you to change the look of one twisted handle spoon from another.

23 Work each trough one more time with a small round gouge to remove any rough ridges left from the rough cutting stage.

24 A final smoothing can be given to your twist troughs by wrapping sandpaper around a pencil, paint brush handle, or small dowel rod.

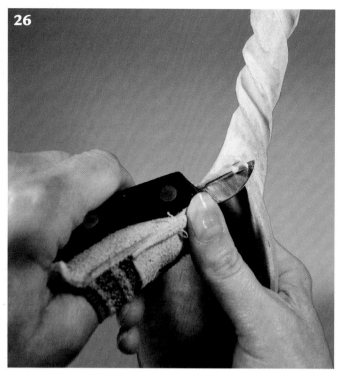

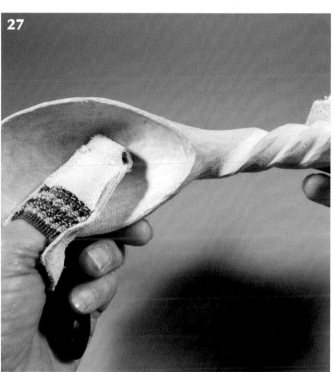

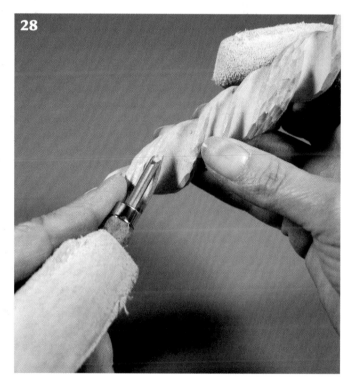

Rounding the edges of the troughs

25–27 With your bench knife, round over the edges of each twist trough. You can lightly round over the edge or carve the edge and flat area between each twist trough into a full curved shape.

28 Take a moment and double check the depth of each of your twist troughs. Use a small round gouge, were necessary, to re-carve any shallow areas.

Note in step 28, I chose to add a little texturing in the large spaces between the twists by cutting small, shallow cuts with my small round gouge. You can add texture between the troughs, inside of the troughs, or work both areas to a smooth finish to add variety to your twist handle spoon carvings.

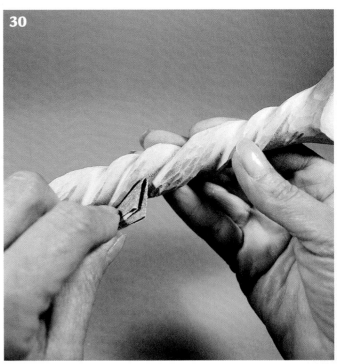

Adding a v-gouge line

29 You can cut a v-gouge line through the center of the largest trough to add a small accent and make it visually different from the two small twist troughs. The v-gouge leaves a thin, sharp angle at the bottom of the trough.

30 Fold a sheet of sandpaper in quarters to dress out the v-gouge cut line. Round over the end of the spoon handle using your bench knife. Complete the smoothing of your bowl and bowl back using a graduation of sandpaper, from 250- to 320-grit. Remove any sanding dust with a clean, dry cloth.

31–32 Apply one or two coats of mineral oil to your completed spoon, allowing each coat to absorb into the wood for about five minutes. Wipe off any excess oil with a clean, dry cloth.

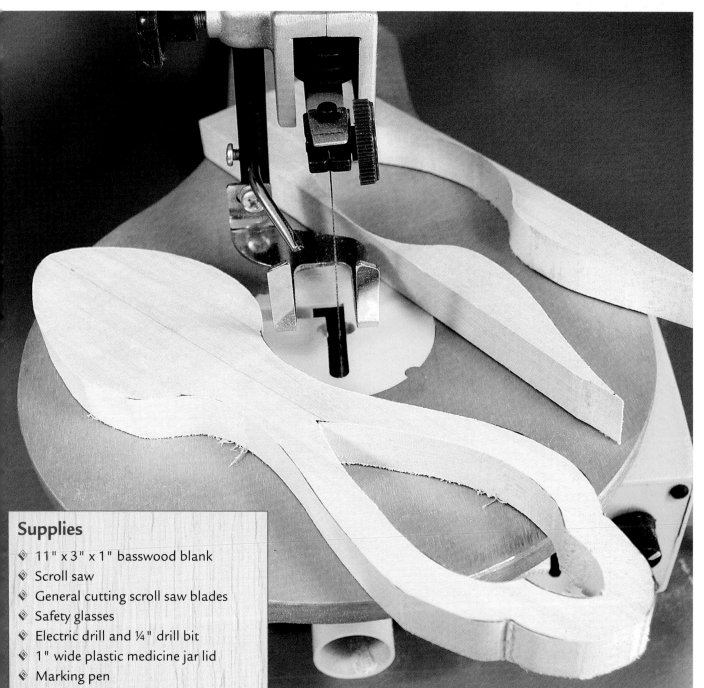

Supplies

- 11" x 3" x 1" basswood blank
- Scroll saw
- General cutting scroll saw blades
- Safety glasses
- Electric drill and ¼" drill bit
- 1" wide plastic medicine jar lid
- Marking pen
- Bench knife
- Medium round gouge
- Wide sweep gouge
- Marking pen or #2 pencil for guide-lines
- 100-, 150-, and 220-grit sandpaper
- Crumpled brown paper bag
- Clean, lint-free tack cloth
- Mineral oil
- Large, soft bristle brush
- Carving gloves
- Large terry-cloth towel

Open Handles

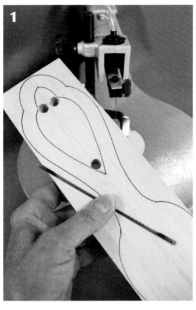

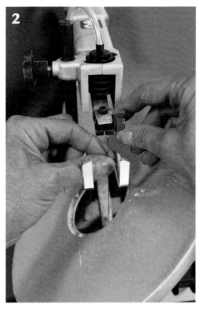

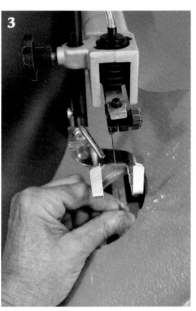

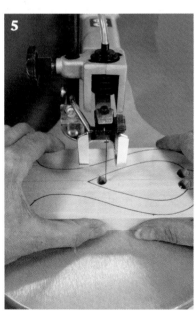

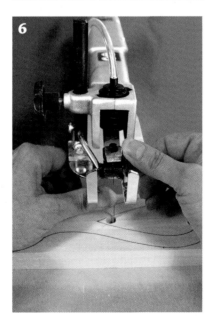

Open designs can be cut into any wide spoon handle pattern, creating an area of visual interest.

Cutting the opening in the handle with a scroll saw or coping saw makes this a quick project.

Cutting the general shape with a scroll saw

1 Begin by reviewing the general instructions for cutting your spoon shape using a scroll saw on pages 18–19. Trace the spoon pattern to your wood blank. With an electric drill and a ¼" drill bit, drill three holes into the open area of the handle as shown in the photo.

2–4 Check your instruction manual on how to remove and replace your scroll saw blade. Follow those directions to remove your blade from the blade holder. Unplug your scroll saw before you change or open your blade.

For my scroll saw, the process of removing the blade begins by removing the throat plate and titling the table to a 45-degree angle. The blade holder on the arm is released. This allows the top edge of the saw blade to be freed from the saw arm.

5–6 Slide the scroll saw blade through one of the drilled holes in the wooden spoon blank. Reset the blade end into the top blade holder and re-tighten the holder. Your scroll saw blade is now inside the hole in the opening, ready to cut the hole line in the spoon. Plug your scroll saw back into your power source to begin cutting.

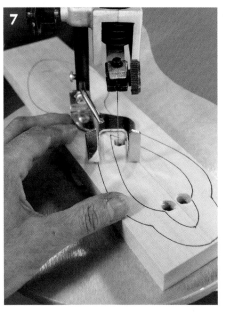

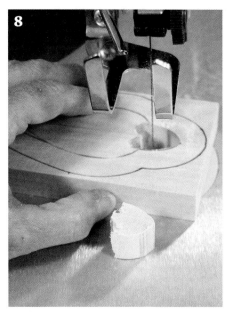

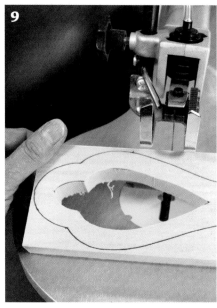

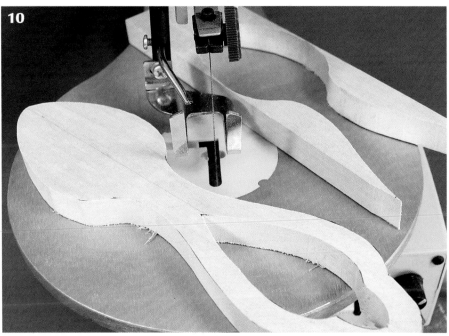

Finishing the scroll saw rough-out

7–9 Cut along the pattern line of the hole opening in your wooden spoon. The two extra holes at the top of the hole area allow you to easily change the direction of your cutting. As you free an area of wood inside the hole area, remove that piece before moving on to cutting the remaining section of hole area.

10 When the hole opening is completely cut, turn off your scroll saw and unplug your machine. Open the blade holder in the arm and slide the wooden spoon off the blade. Return the blade tip to the holder and re-tighten the holder. Finish cutting your spoon by working along the outside pattern line of the spoon.

Drainage holes

11 You can use an electric drill to cut your drainage holes and the top and bottom holes for your slots or fork tines.

Drill bits can chip out the bottom or underside of the drilled wood, so do your drilling from the back of the spoon into the front bowl area where you will be carving away the extra wood that might get chipped.

Drill any holes during the rough-cut stage of your spoon carving.

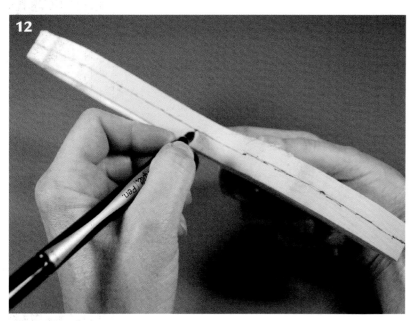

Marking your guidelines

12 Measure the thickness of your rough-cut spoon and make several marks on the side at one-half the thickness.

13 On the front of the rough-cut spoon mark a line about ⅜" from the bowl and handle joint in the bowl area. Mark a second line about ⅜" from the cut point of the open hole on the handle side of the joint.

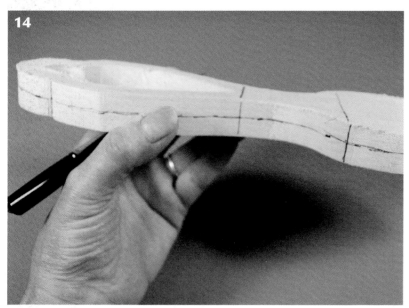

14 Extend the lines marked in step 13 along both sides of the rough-cut spoon.

15 On the sides of the spoon mark a diagonal line from the center line, marked in step 12, in the bowl area to the front edge of the side at the handle line mark. Mark a second line in the same area, working from the bottom edge of the rough cut in the bowl area to the center line mark in the handle area.

These two lines, on each side, mark the slant of the handle and bowl joint. With your marking pen make small x's to note which areas of the wood blank you will be removing—this is the upper section in the bowl area and the lower section in the handle area.

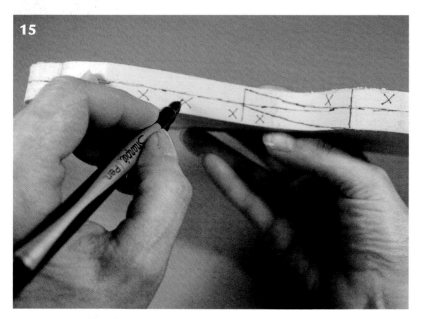

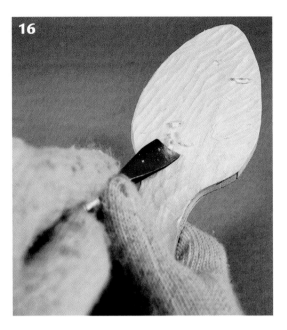

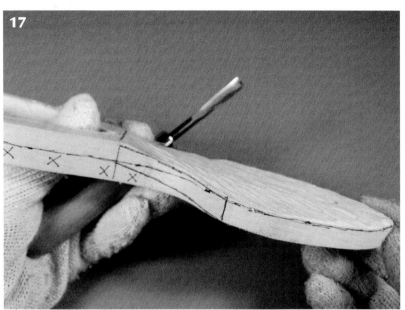

Cutting the handle and bowl slant

16–17 With a medium round gouge and a wide sweep gouge, cut away the excess wood on the top of the rough cut in the bowl area, following your guidelines along the side of the spoon.

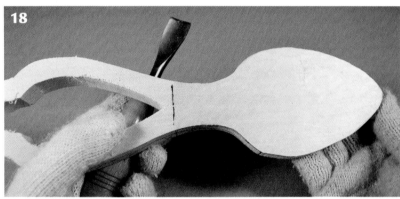

18 Re-work this area with the wide sweep gouge to smooth the bowl area and remove any rough gouge ridges.

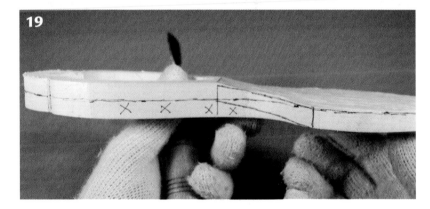

19–20 Turn your rough-cut blank over so that you are working on the back side of the spoon. Repeat steps 16–18 to remove the excess wood in the handle side of the spoon.

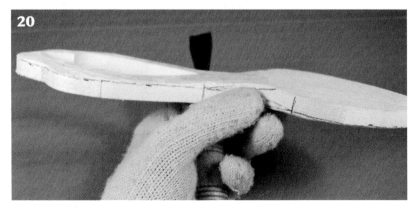

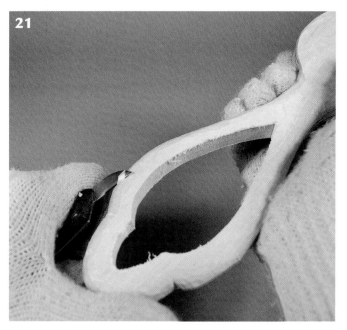

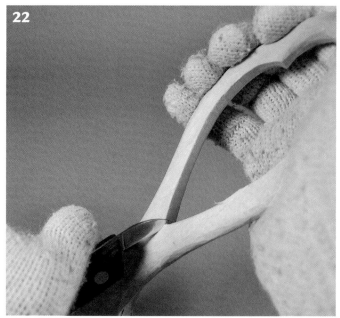

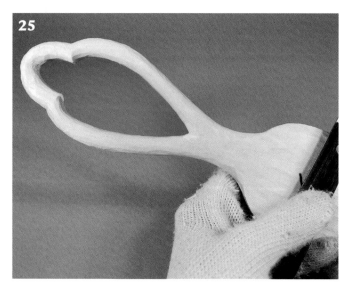

Rounding the open hole in the handle

21 With your bench knife, round over the outer edges of your spoon handle on both the front and the back.

22 Begin the rounding over of the opening in the handle by making a straight cut into the wood at the point of the opening.

23–25 As you round over the inside edge of the opening, you can work your bench knife cuts into the slice made in step 22 to round the inside edge of the point.

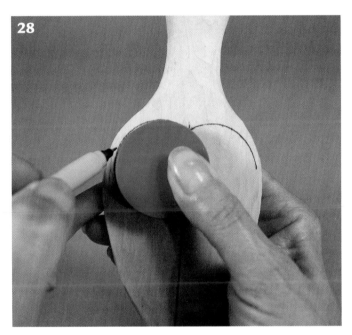

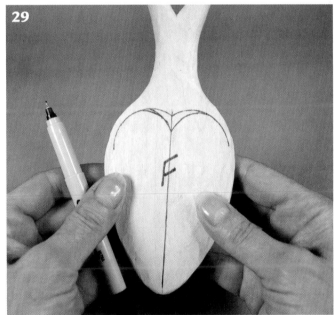

Rounding over the back of the spoon bowl

26 Mark you guidelines for the cutting direction of the wood grain onto your spoon bowl back. With a bench knife, round over the edges of the spoon bowl.

Because this spoon is wide from edge to edge but thin in the depth of the wood, the center area of the bowl remains at the original flat surface of the blank.

27 Taper the back of the bowl into the handle joint using your wide sweep gouge.

Marking the heart-shaped bowl

28 The front of the bowl for this Wedding Spoon is heart shaped. With your marking pen, make a guideline through the center of the bowl area.

29 Lay a 1" wide medicine bottle lid against the wood and position at the top of the bowl, ⅛" away from the bowl and handle joint edge. Trace along the jar lid with a marking pen. Slide the plastic jar lid to the opposite side of the center guideline and draw around the lid to create the second half of the heart's top edge.

With your marking pen, mark a small tight arc on each side of the top of your plastic cap circles to create the center point of the heart shape.

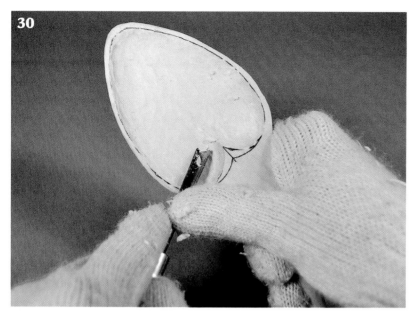

Cutting the heart-shaped bowl

30 Working with a medium round gouge or a bent gouge, begin the cutting of your bowl at the top of the heart, working your cutting strokes towards the center of the bowl.

Work each arc area of the heart independently as if each was an individual bowl top. This will leave a small v-shaped point at the top of the heart in the bowl and handle joint area.

31 Use your bench knife to round over both the inside and outside edges of the bowl.

32 Because my open-handle spoon will be decorative, I chose to allow the medium gouge cutting strokes to remain inside of my bowl area. This accents the bowl area with a deep texture that compliments the bench knife cut strokes of the handle.

Lightly sand the entire spoon to remove just the sharp, hard edges left from the rough-out cutting. Remove any sanding dust with a dry, lint-free cloth

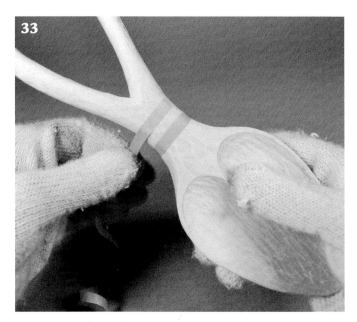

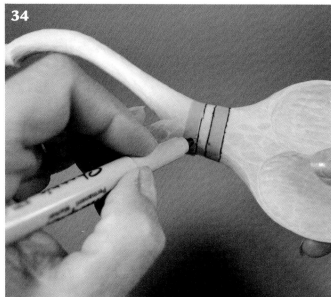

Adding accent lines to the handle

33–34 Cut two pieces of painter's tape—one ¼" wide by 6" long and one ⅜" by 6" long.

Lay the ⅜" wide piece of tape onto the handle at the narrowest point in the handle, about ½" above the bowl. Roll the tape around the handle until it meets the beginning of the tape. Cut off the excess tape and press the tape firmly against the wood.

Roll the second ¼" wide strip of tape around the handle about ¼" above the first. Cut off the excess and press into place.

Work your marking pen along the outside edge of both sides of the ⅜" wide tape. Mark along the bottom edge of the ¼" wide strip of tape. Remove both pieces of painter's tape. This will leave you with three cutting guidelines at your bowl and handle joint area.

35–36 Use your bench knife to cut a v-trough line following each of the bowl and handle joint guidelines. This is a two-stroke cut. Hold your bench knife vertical to the guideline (photo 35) along the outer edge of the guideline ink mark. Then tilt the angle of the top edge of the knife slightly away from the line to be cut (photo 36). Push the knife into the wood.

37 The second stroke is worked on the opposite side of the marking line. Turn your spoon around in your hand and repeat the cutting stroke. This will lift a small v-shaped chip from the line. Work the line in small sections to create a textured line full of small straight planes. Work all three bowl and handle joint accent lines.

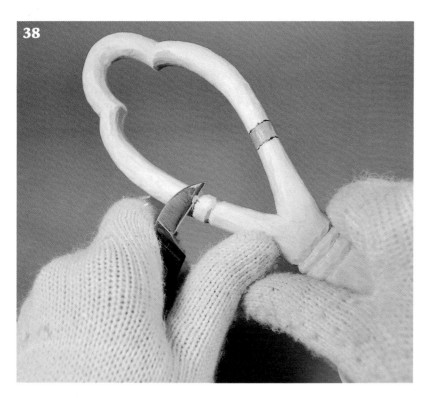

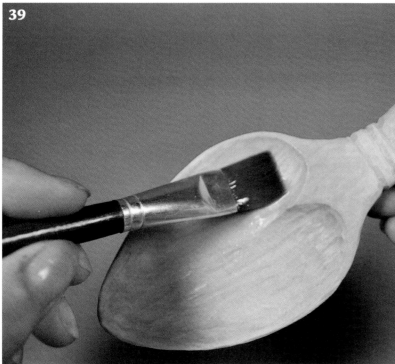

Adding more accent lines

38 Work another set of accent lines around the open arms of the handle area. Use a strip of painter's tape that has been cut to ¼" wide by 6" long for each.

39 Lightly sand your entire spoon with 320-grit sandpaper. Work the sandpaper to remove just the roughest ridges, leaving as much carving texture as possible in your spoon. Remove any sanding dust with a dry, clean cloth.

Apply one to two coats of mineral oil to the entire spoon. Allow each coat to soak into the wood for about five minutes. Wipe any excess oil off the spoon with a dry, clean cloth.

Supplies

- 12" x 5" x ½" basswood blank
- Coping saw / miter saw
- Safety glasses
- Non-skid kitchen mat
- Clamps
- Marking pen
- Bench knife
- Medium round gouge
- Wide sweep gouge
- Marking pen or #2 pencil for guidelines
- 100-, 150-, and 220-grit sandpaper
- Crumpled brown paper bag
- Clean, lint-free tack cloth
- Mineral oil
- Large, soft bristle brush
- Carving gloves
- Large terry-cloth towel

Wedding Spoons

There is a wide variety of styles of Wedding Spoons, yet traditionally each one was created as a gift from the man to his beloved as a token of his intentions to marry her. In this section we will work through two Scandinavian-styled wedding spoon designs. Most wedding spoons are worked from thin stock, ¾" to ½", with flat backs.

Chip-Carved Wedding Spoon

Trimming the sides

1 Once you have used the coping saw to create a rough cut (see pages 16–17), you can begin to use your bench knife to remove any rough-cut areas left from the coping saw process. Check that your side walls are straight and square to the front surface of your spoon blank.

Tapering the sides of the handle

2 With your ruler and marking pen, make a straight line through the center of your handle. Mark guidelines on the handle at the widest point in the handle just as you would mark the back of your spoon bowl. During the next few steps we will be tapering the handle sides away from the center guideline to create an inverted v-shape for the handle area.

3 Using a wide sweep gouge and working from the center guideline, taper the handle's top surface down towards the sides of the handle. The center line of the handle remains at the ½" thickness of the wood and the sides are lowered to measure ¼".

The side tapering stops where the handle narrows and becomes the handle and bowl joint.

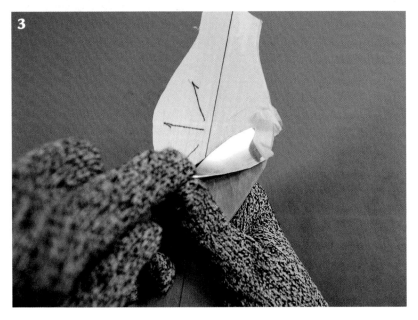

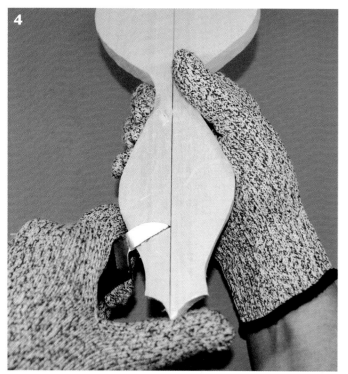

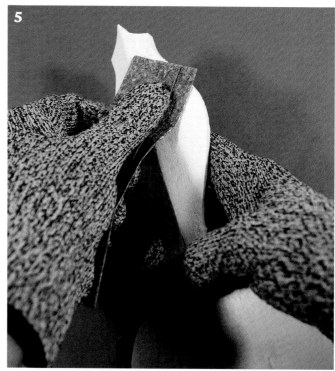

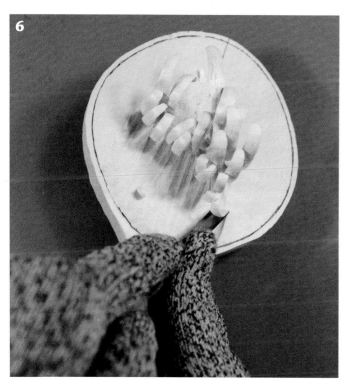

Smooth the handle taper

4-5 Use your bench knife to smooth the wide sweep gouge ridges. Use 150- and 220-grit sandpaper to lightly sand your handle to smooth the tapered sides.

Rounding the bowl

6-7 Mark a guideline around the outer edge of the bowl about ⅛" from the edge. Use your medium and wide sweep gouge to round the center section of your bowl. This area has just a minor dip to create the bowl shape. Shave the rough ridges left from the bowl shaping by holding your wide sweep gouge at a low angle to the wood to cut very thin slivers.

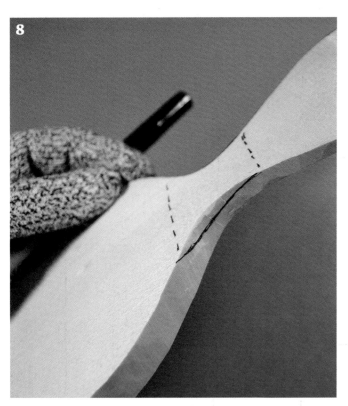

Curving the back bowl and handle joint

8 Mark a guideline 1" above and below the tightest point in the width of the bowl and handle joint. On the sides of the spoon, mark a small curve that connects the two guidelines and that curves to meet the halfway point in the side thickness.

9-10 Use your wide sweep gouge to cut the handle and bowl joint curve, using the guidelines for your position. Taper this curve gently on both sides of the spoon—the handle side and the bowl side.

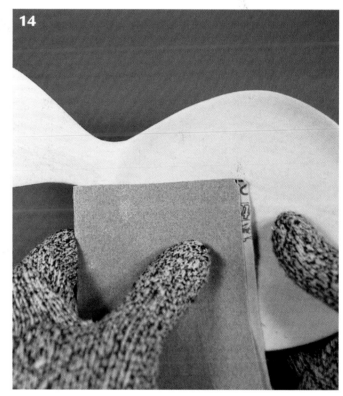

Round over the side edges of your spoon

11 Using your bench knife, round over the edges of the spoon bowl back. The large, center section of the bowl remains at the original flatness of the wood blank.

12 Round over the sides of the handle back using your bench knife.

13 Lightly shave all edges of your spoon by holding the bench knife low to the wood and taking very thin cuts.

14 Using a graduation of sandpaper, from 150- to 320-grit, sand your spoon. Remove any sanding dust using a dry, clean cloth.

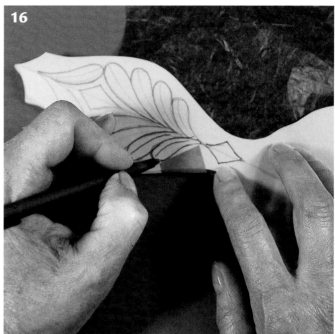

Tracing the chip-carving pattern

15–16 Make a copy of the chip-carving pattern onto computer paper or vellum. Cut the pattern along the spoon edge guidelines. Rub the back of the pattern with a soft, #4 – #6, pencil. Tape the patterns onto your spoon handle with the pencil rubbed side against the wood. Using an ink pen, trace along the pattern lines. Remove the pattern paper and tape.

17 As a general habit, I do a practice board for any of my chip-carving patterns before I begin work on my project. In this sample I have traced the handle chip-carving pattern several times to a matching piece of ½" stock basswood. I can practice my cuts and pattern before I move onto my spoon.

Cutting the leaf chips

18–19 Each leaf shape is created by combining two chip-carving cuts. Each chip-carving cut is created using two strokes. Using a large chip-carving knife, the first cut of the chip is made along the center line of the leaf shape chip with the knife held in a vertical position. As you pull your chip knife through the line, the tip begins high in the wood, dips to its deepest point at the center of the line, and then lifts out of the wood at the opposite end of the line cut.

20–21 Reverse the spoon in your hand. Angle your bench knife towards the first cut and begin cutting the second stroke by following the outside chip pattern line. Again, begin with just the tip of the knife in the wood at the first point of the line. As you pull your knife, slowly drop it deeper into the wood. When you reach the center of the line, begin lifting the blade tip out of the wood.

22 This two-stroke cut releases half of the leaf shape. Repeat for each remaining leaf shape pattern area.

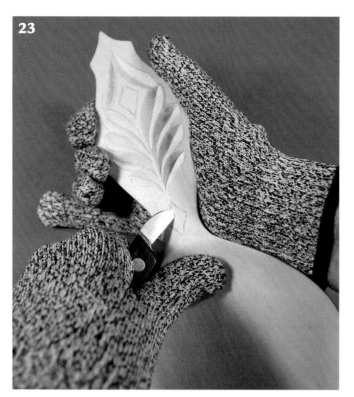

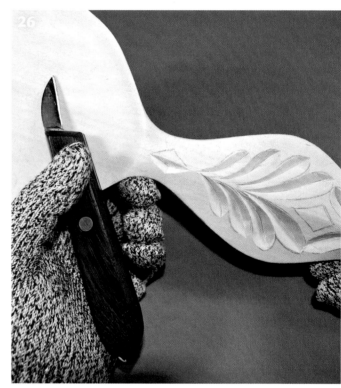

Double-triangle chips

23–26 The double-triangle designs above and below the leaf patterns are also cut as two separate chip carvings. Begin by setting your blade point at the end of one triangle pattern line. Angle the blade towards the center of the triangle. Pull the cut. Begin the cut high in the wood, slowly deepen your blade as you reach the center of the line, then raise the tip out of the wood as you near the end of the line. Repeat this step for the remaining two lines of the triangle pattern. This will release a small triangle of wood. Repeat for the remaining triangle chips.

Completing the spoon

27 Take a moment and double-check that your chip-carving areas are even in size, slope, and have no areas that need a little fine tuning.

28 Lightly sand the chip-carved area of your handle using 320-grit sandpaper to remove any remaining pattern tracing lines. Remove the sanding dust using a dry, clean cloth.

29 Finish your spoon with one to two coats of mineral oil. Allow each coat to soak into the wood for about five minutes, then wipe off any excess oil.

Cut-Work Wedding Spoon

Cutting the rough spoon

1–2 There are two small changes between the Chip-Carved Wedding Spoon and the Cut-Work Wedding Spoon that turns this project into a unique spoon. We will change the chip-carving pattern and we will angle the handle back to thin the wood for up-end gouge cutting.

Follow the directions for the Chip-Carved Wedding Spoon from step 1 through 23 to create, shape, and sand your general wedding spoon.

Angling the handle back

3 Mark a guideline down the center line of the back of the handle. Use a medium or wide sweep gouge to cut along the back, working from the outer edge towards the center guideline.

Taper the center of the back to match the taper you created on the front of the handle, so that each area of the handle is only ¼" thick.

Use your bench knife to cut free the round gouge strokes.

4–5 Use the wide sweep gouge to shave the back taper to an even, smooth surface.

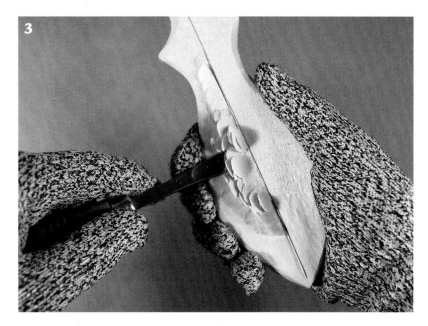

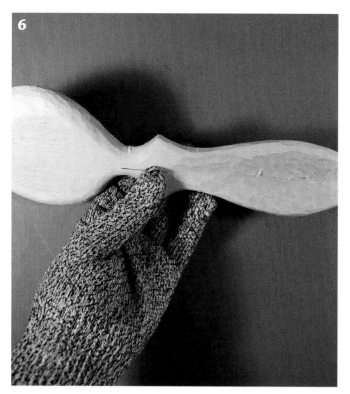

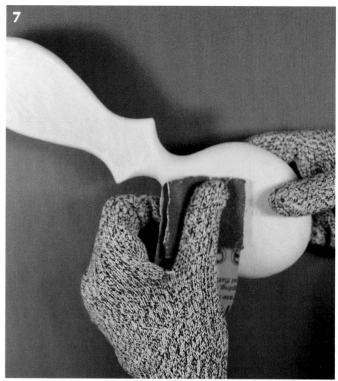

Smooth and sand the back handle taper

6–7 When you have completed the shaving step with the wide round gouge, sand the back handle with a graduation of sandpapers, from 150- to 320-grit. Remove any sanding dust with a dry, clean cloth.

Trace the chip pattern

8–9 Make a copy of the chip-carving pattern on a piece of computer paper or vellum. Cut the pattern along the outside spoon lines.

Rub the back of your pattern with a soft, #4 – #6, pencil. Position the pattern over the handle and tape into place. Trace along the pattern lines with an ink pen.

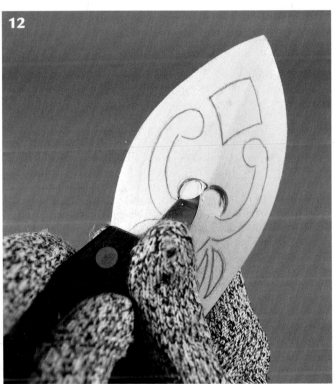

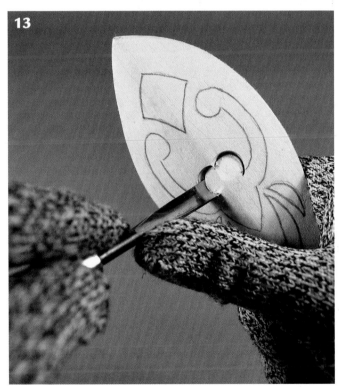

Up-ending your round gouge

10–13 Up-end a medium, straight round gouge over one of the circles at the top of the open cut-out portion of the design. Roll the gouge in your fingers, slowly cutting a thin-line circle into the wood.

Repeat the up-end gouge work in the second circle of the pattern, cutting it to the same depth as the first.

Use your bench knife to slice free the areas you have up-end cut.

Work these steps several times until you have almost cut the circles free from the wood.

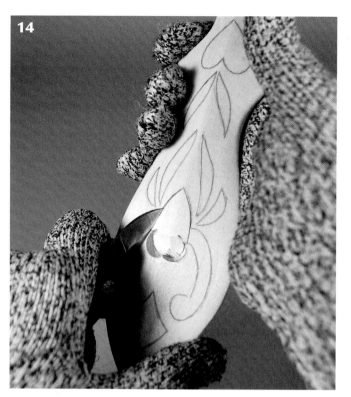

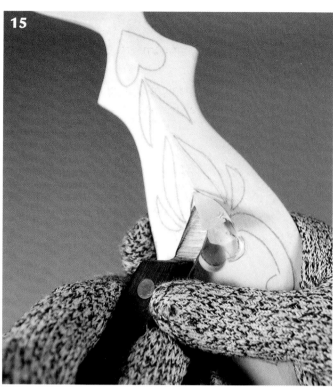

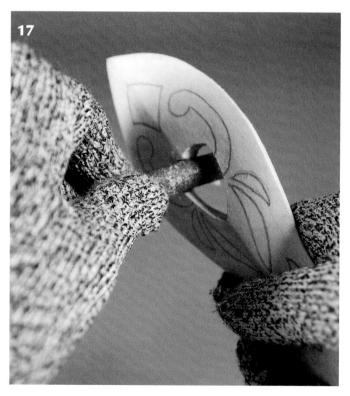

Cutting the sides of the open heart

14–15 Use your bench knife to cut along the sides of the heart pattern, connecting the bench knife cuts to the up-end cuts worked in the previous steps. Use your bench knife to slice free the cut area of the heart. Continue cutting the heart with the up-end gouge cuts and side cuts with the bench knife until you have freed and released all of the wood in the heart area.

16 Use your bench knife to smooth the inside walls of the heart.

17 Wrap 220-grit sandpaper around a pencil and sand the inside walls of the heart.

Freeing the heart arm holes

18–20 The two arms that come off the center heart shape end in a circular pattern. Up-end your medium, straight round gouge and cut these circles free from the wood.

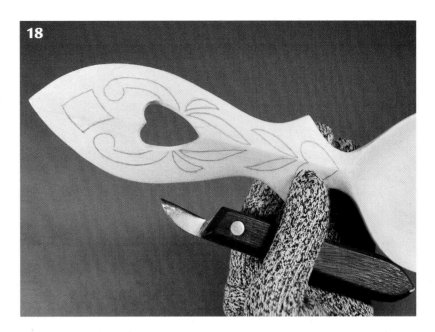

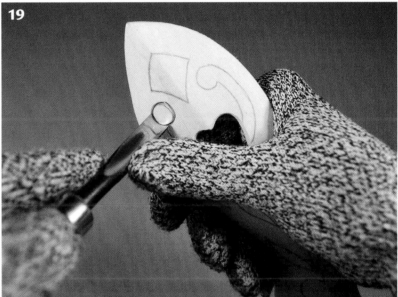

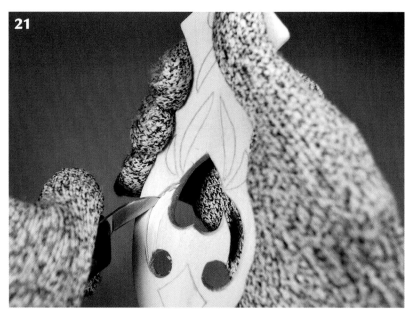

Cutting the heart side arms

21 With your bench knife, cut along one side of one of the side arms, connecting the cut between the heart shape and the arm's end circles.

22 Re-cut this line with the bench knife, slightly angling the blade away from the first cut to create a v-trough cut.

23 Repeat these two steps on both sides of the arms to free the arms from the wood.

Use your bench knife to smooth the inside walls of the arms.

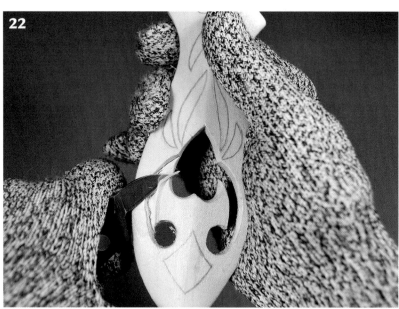

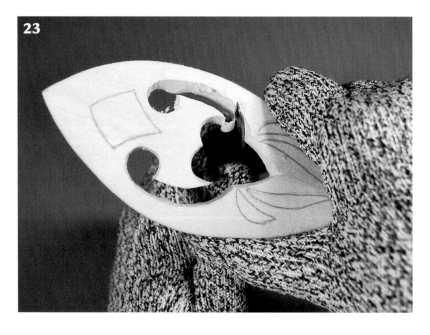

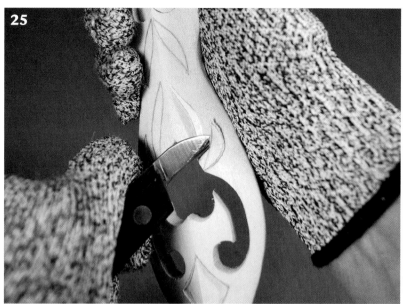

Chip carve the remaining pattern

24–25 The leaf-shaped chips are cut in two strokes. Begin with your bench knife at the point of one line of the leaf. Angle the blade towards the center line of the leaf. As you pull the stroke, slowly deepen your cut to the center of the leaf. As you pull away from the center, slowly raise the knife until your reach the second point.

Repeat this stroke for the second side of the leaf to free the chip from the wood.

Work the double triangles and the small heart pattern in the same manner.

26 Lightly sand your spoon to remove any remaining pattern tracing lines. Remove any sanding dust with a dry, clean cloth.

27 Apply one to two coats of mineral oil to the entire spoon. Allow each coat to soak into the wood for five minutes, then wipe off any excess oil.

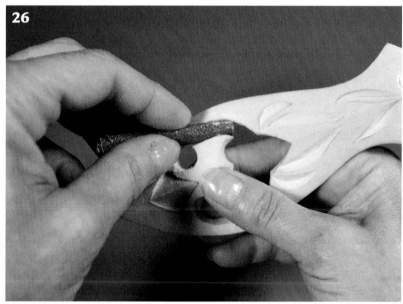

Project Patterns

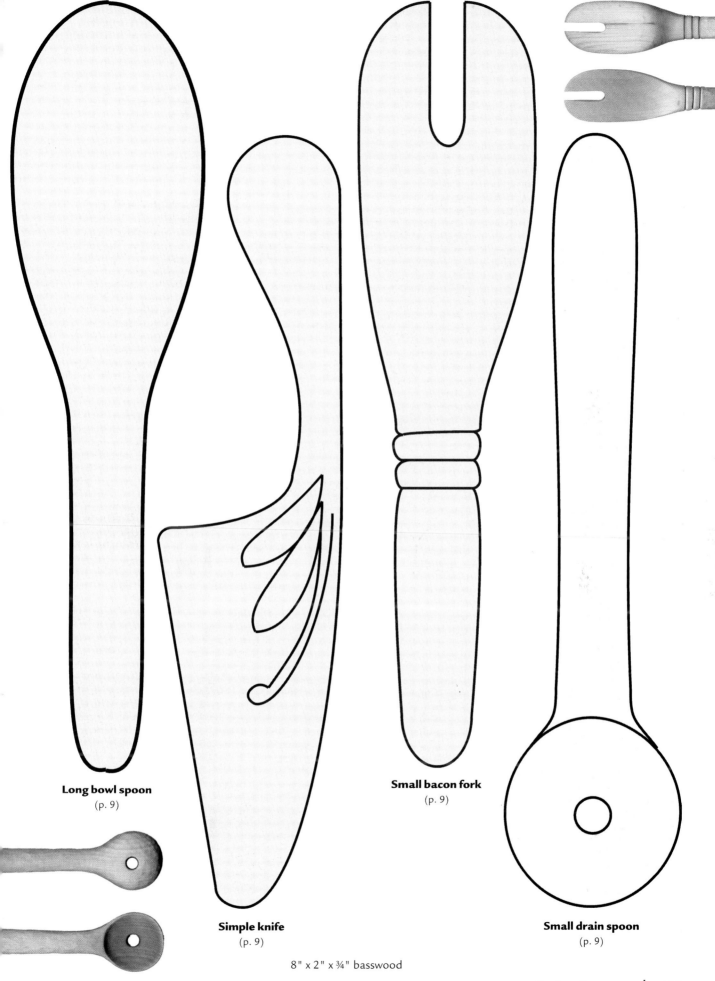

Long bowl spoon
(p. 9)

Simple knife
(p. 9)

8" x 2" x ¾" basswood

Small bacon fork
(p. 9)

Small drain spoon
(p. 9)

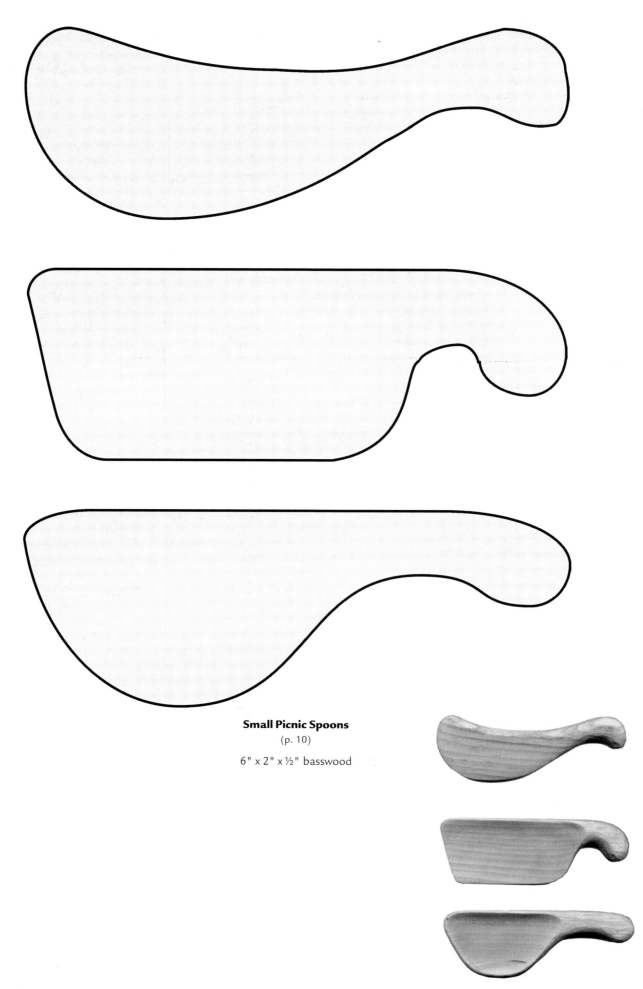

Small Picnic Spoons
(p. 10)

6" x 2" x ½" basswood

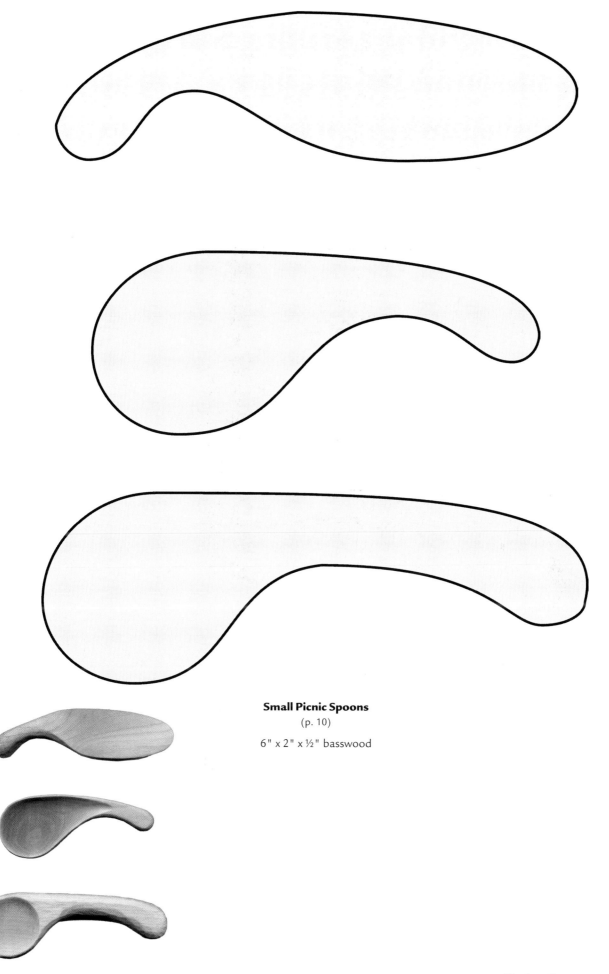

Small Picnic Spoons
(p. 10)

6" x 2" x ½" basswood

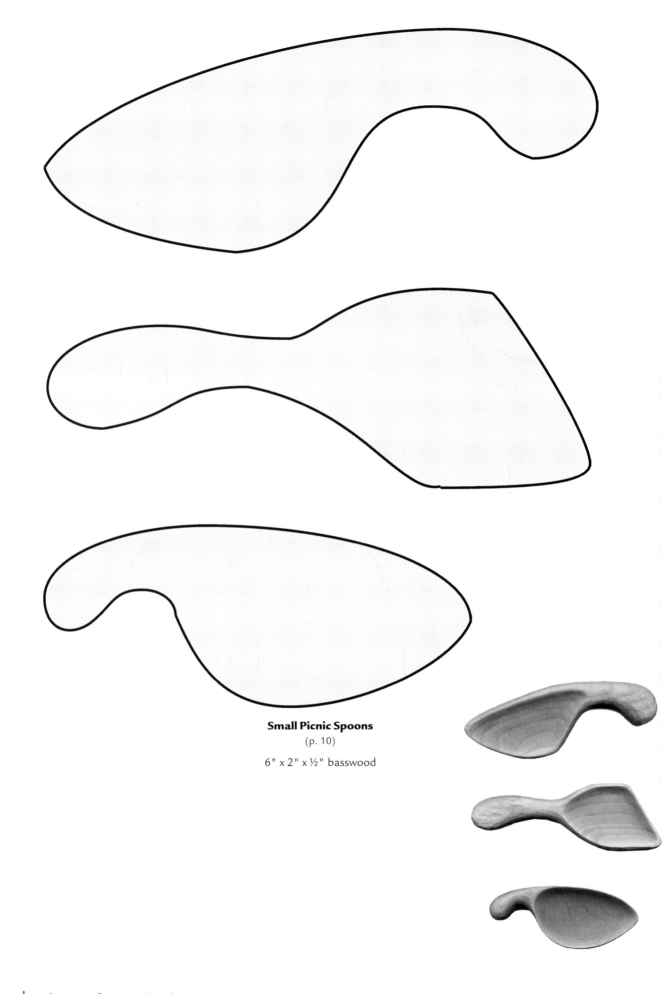

Small Picnic Spoons
(p. 10)

6" x 2" x ½" basswood

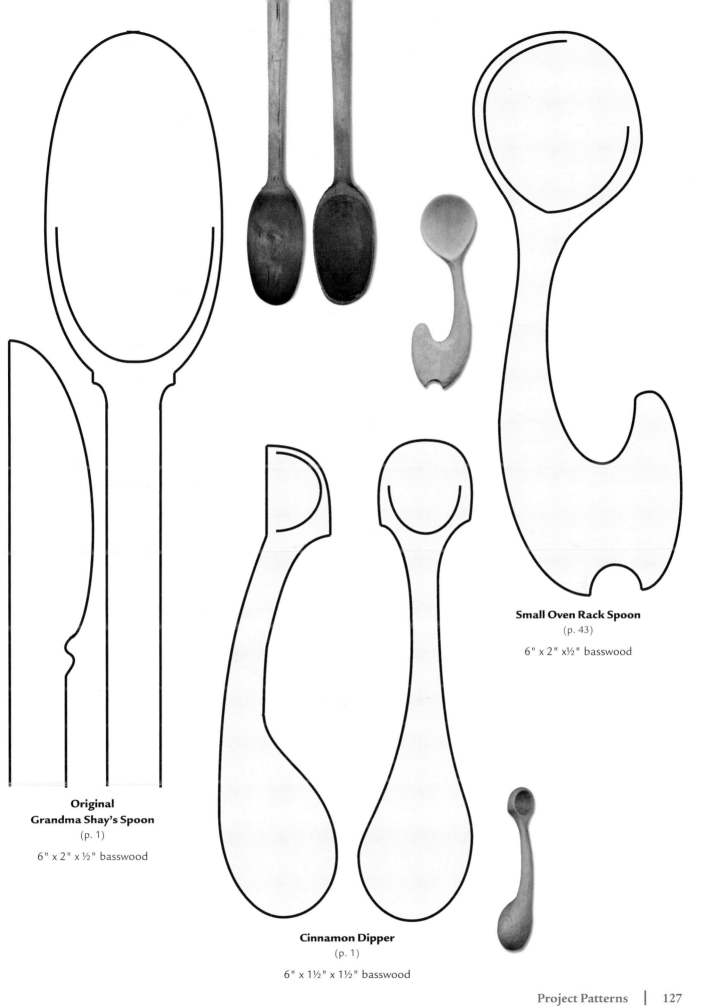

**Original
Grandma Shay's Spoon**
(p. 1)

6" x 2" x ½" basswood

Cinnamon Dipper
(p. 1)

6" x 1½" x 1½" basswood

Small Oven Rack Spoon
(p. 43)

6" x 2" x½" basswood

Grandma Shay's Spoon Project
(p. 22)

12-14" x 3" x 1" basswood blank

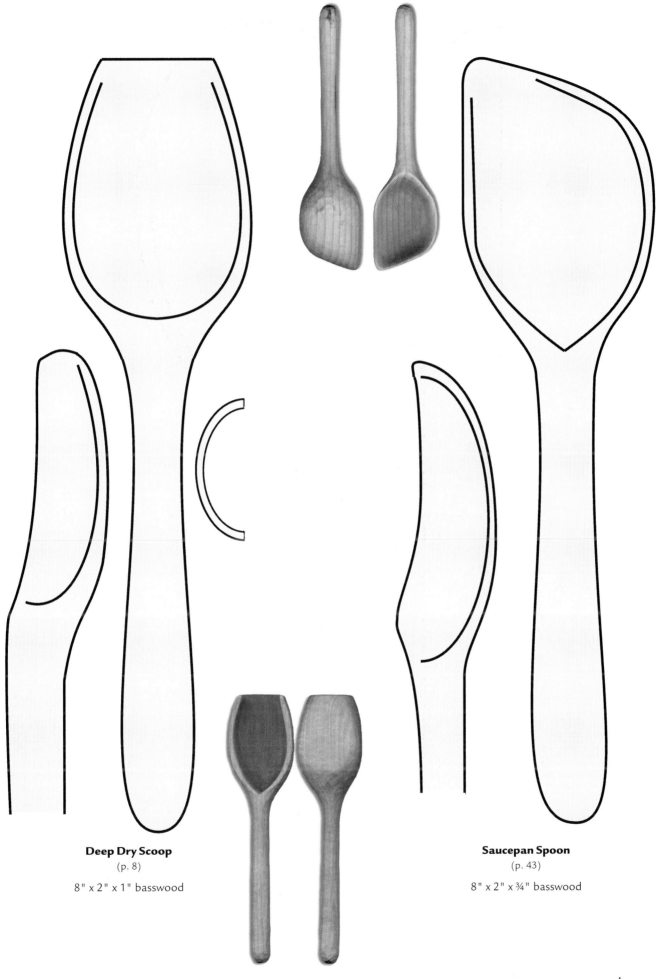

Deep Dry Scoop
(p. 8)

8" x 2" x 1" basswood

Saucepan Spoon
(p. 43)

8" x 2" x ¾" basswood

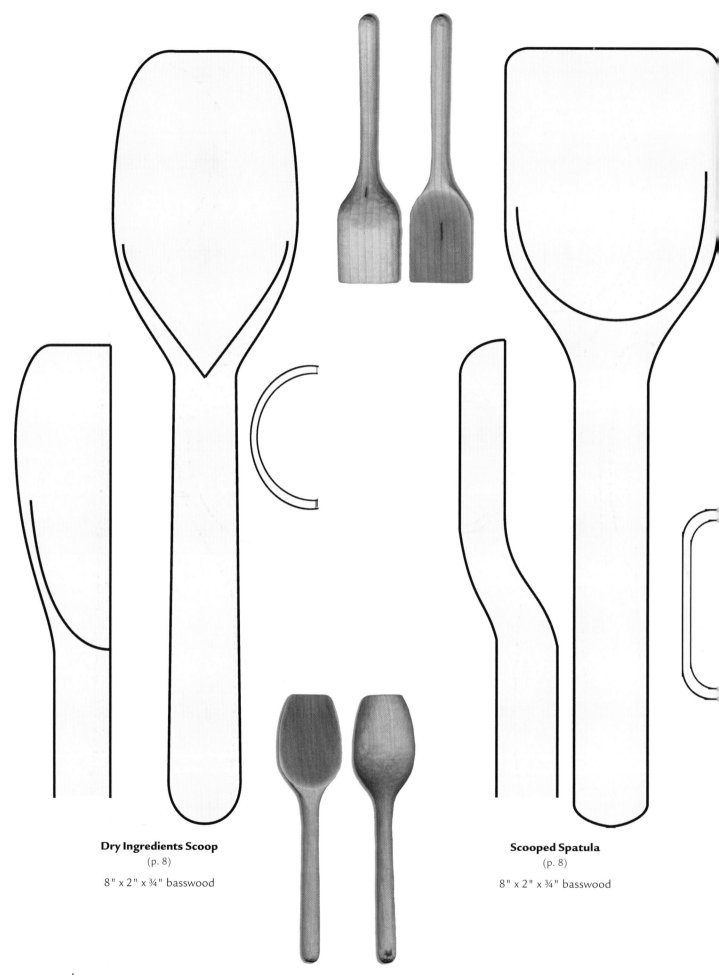

Dry Ingredients Scoop
(p. 8)

8" x 2" x ¾" basswood

Scooped Spatula
(p. 8)

8" x 2" x ¾" basswood

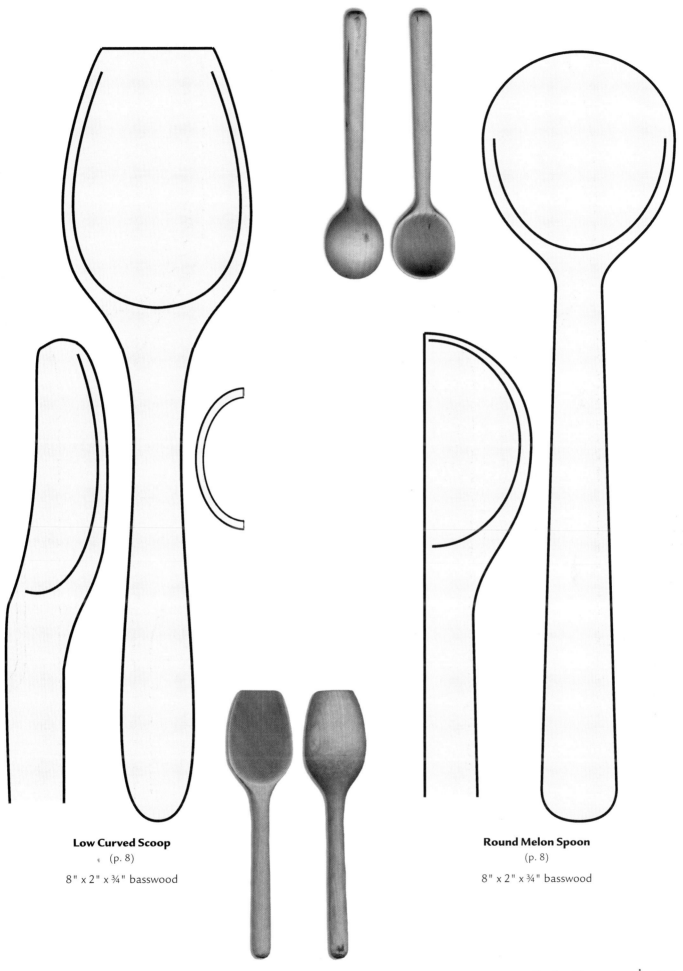

Low Curved Scoop
(p. 8)

8" x 2" x ¾" basswood

Round Melon Spoon
(p. 8)

8" x 2" x ¾" basswood

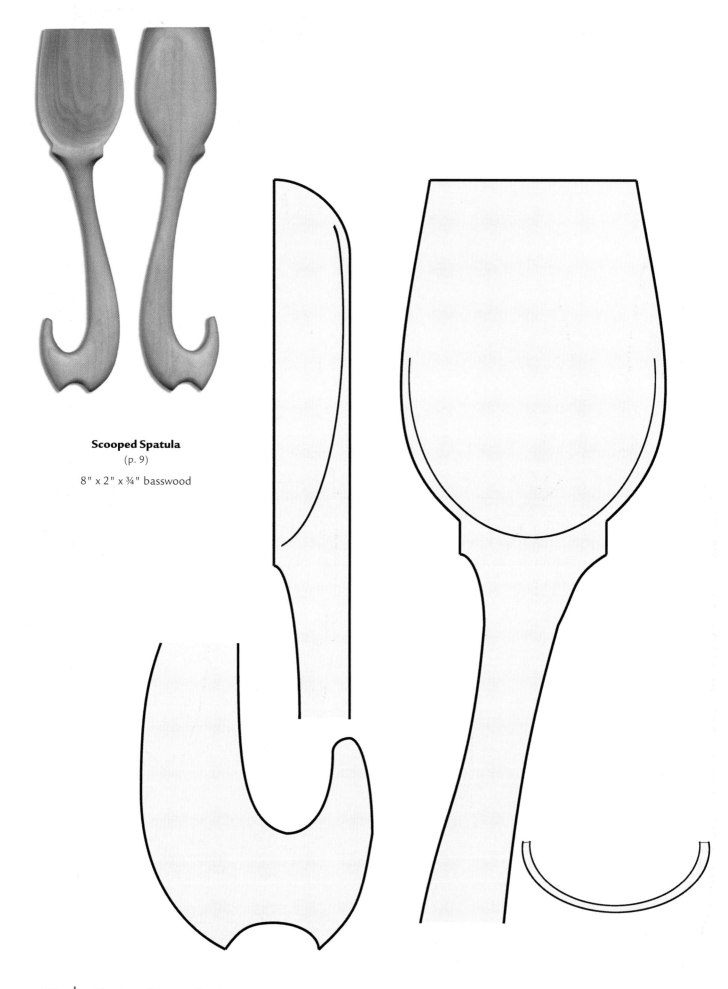

Scooped Spatula
(p. 9)

8" x 2" x ¾" basswood

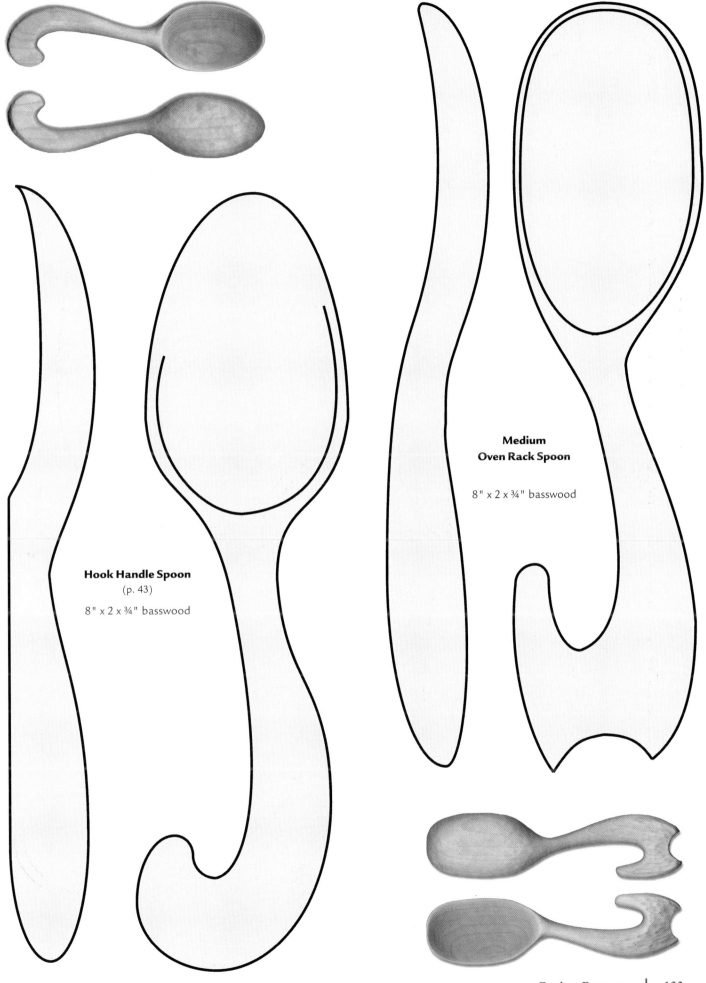

Hook Handle Spoon
(p. 43)

8" x 2 x ¾" basswood

**Medium
Oven Rack Spoon**

8" x 2 x ¾" basswood

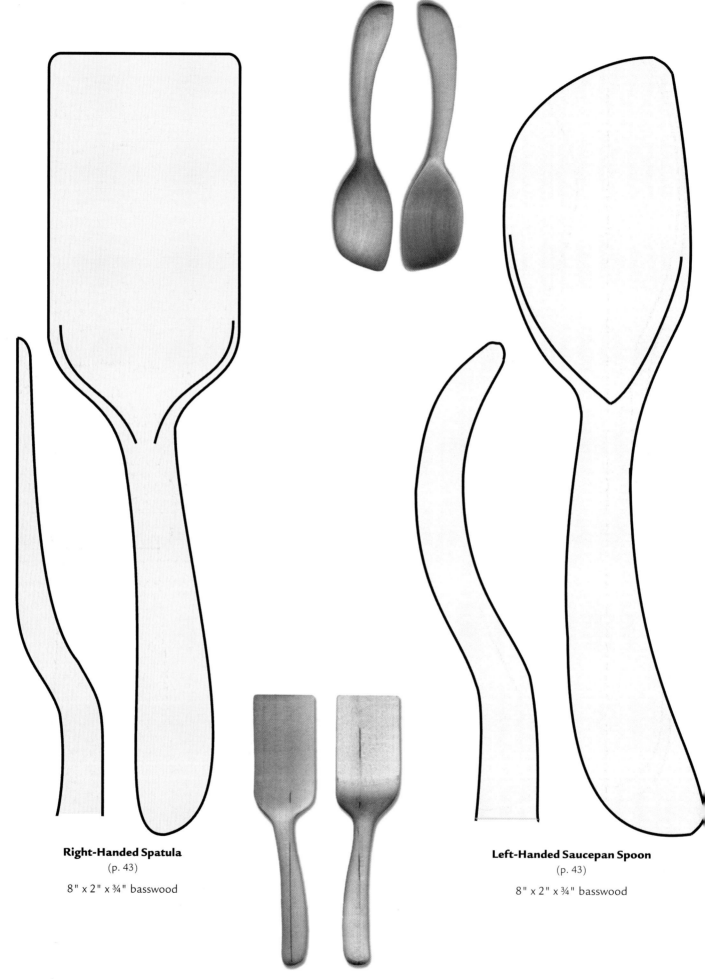

Right-Handed Spatula
(p. 43)

8" x 2" x ¾" basswood

Left-Handed Saucepan Spoon
(p. 43)

8" x 2" x ¾" basswood

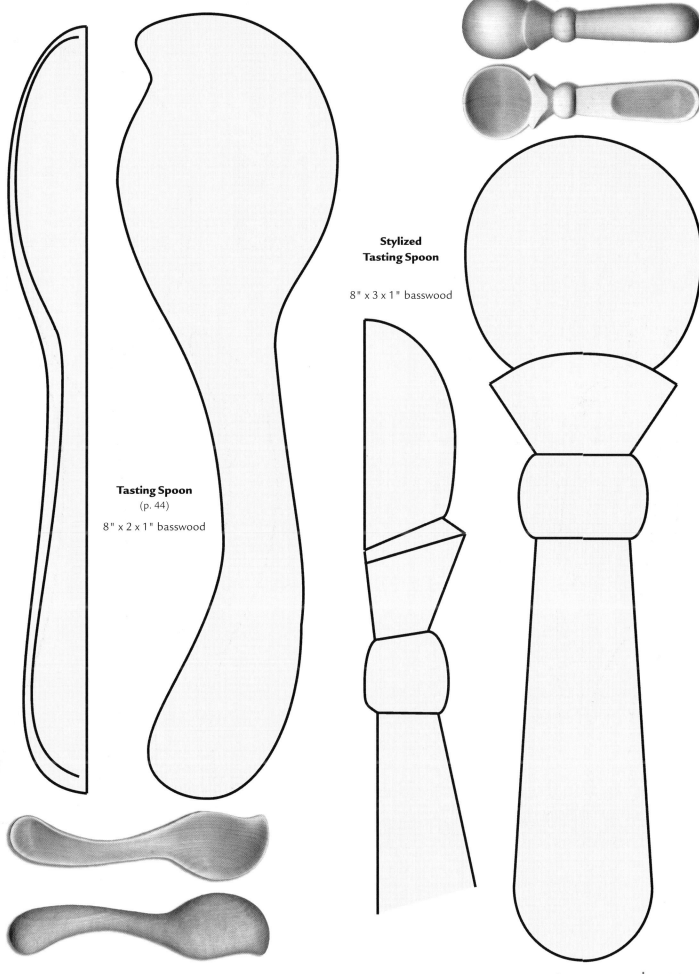

Tasting Spoon
(p. 44)

8" x 2 x 1" basswood

**Stylized
Tasting Spoon**

8" x 3 x 1" basswood

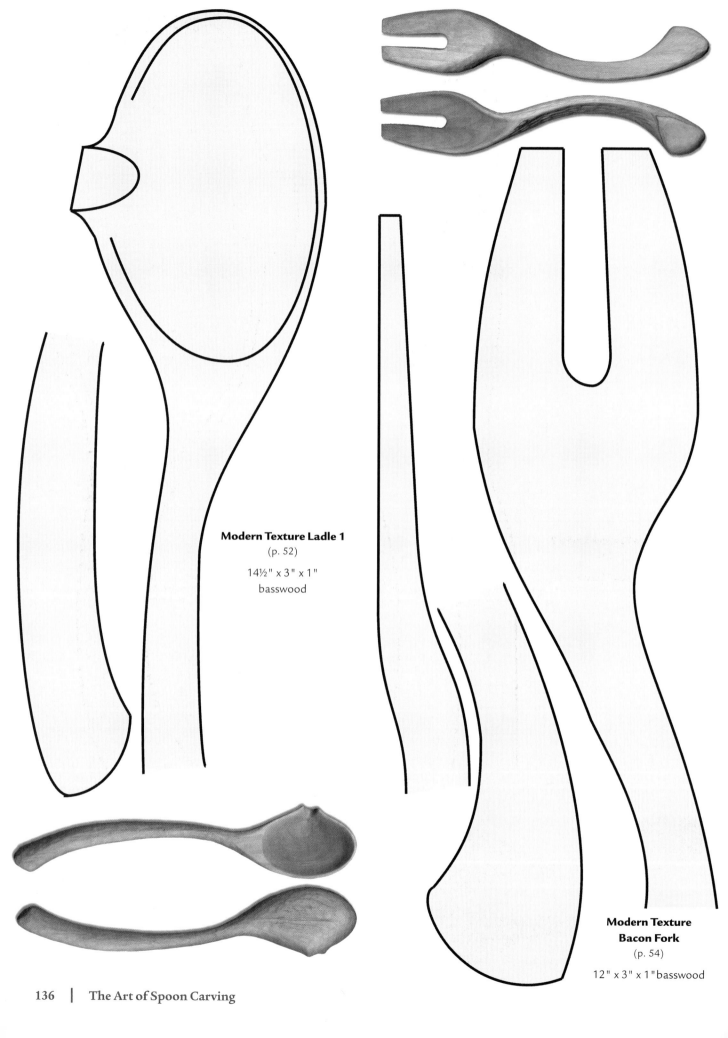

Modern Texture Ladle 1
(p. 52)

14½" x 3" x 1"
basswood

**Modern Texture
Bacon Fork**
(p. 54)

12" x 3" x 1" basswood

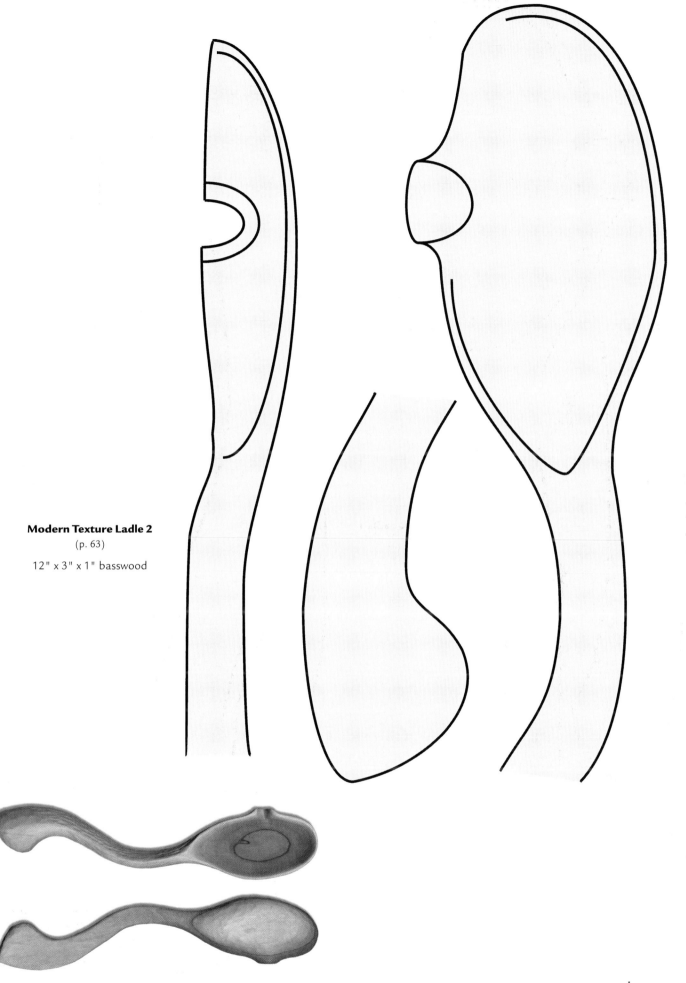

Modern Texture Ladle 2
(p. 63)

12" x 3" x 1" basswood

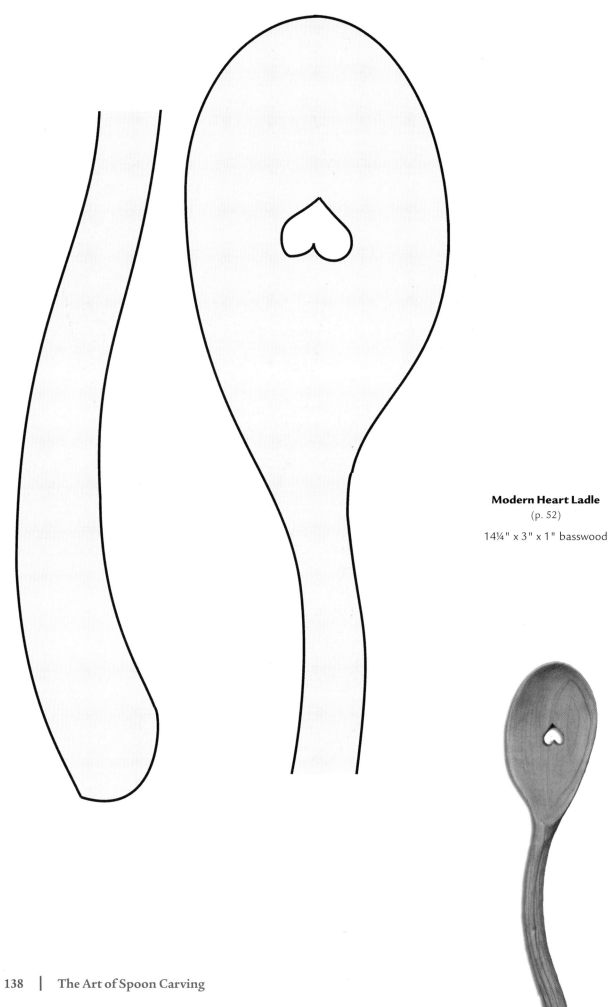

Modern Heart Ladle
(p. 52)

14¼" x 3" x 1" basswood

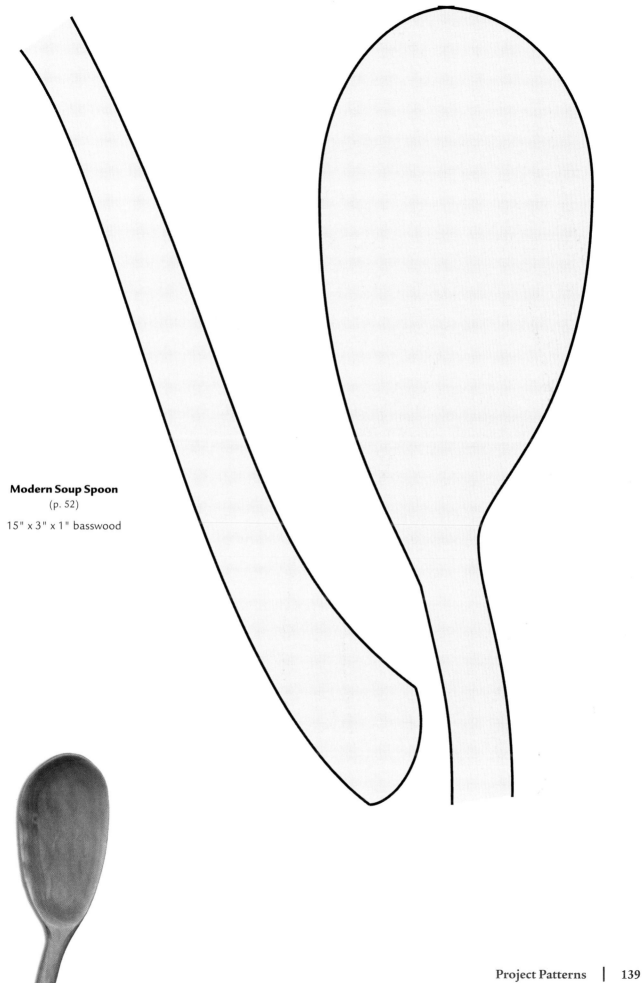

Modern Soup Spoon
(p. 52)

15" x 3" x 1" basswood

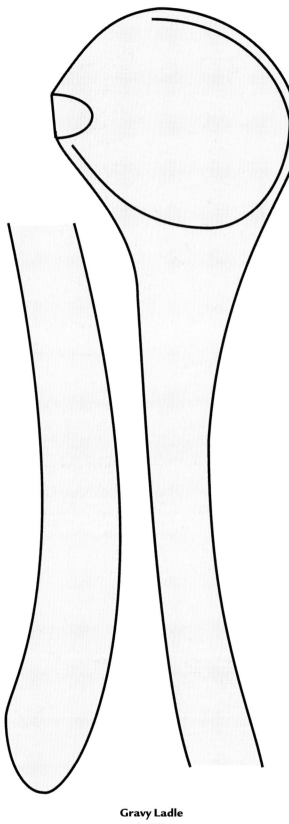

Gravy Ladle
(p. 52)

14" x 2½" x 1" basswood

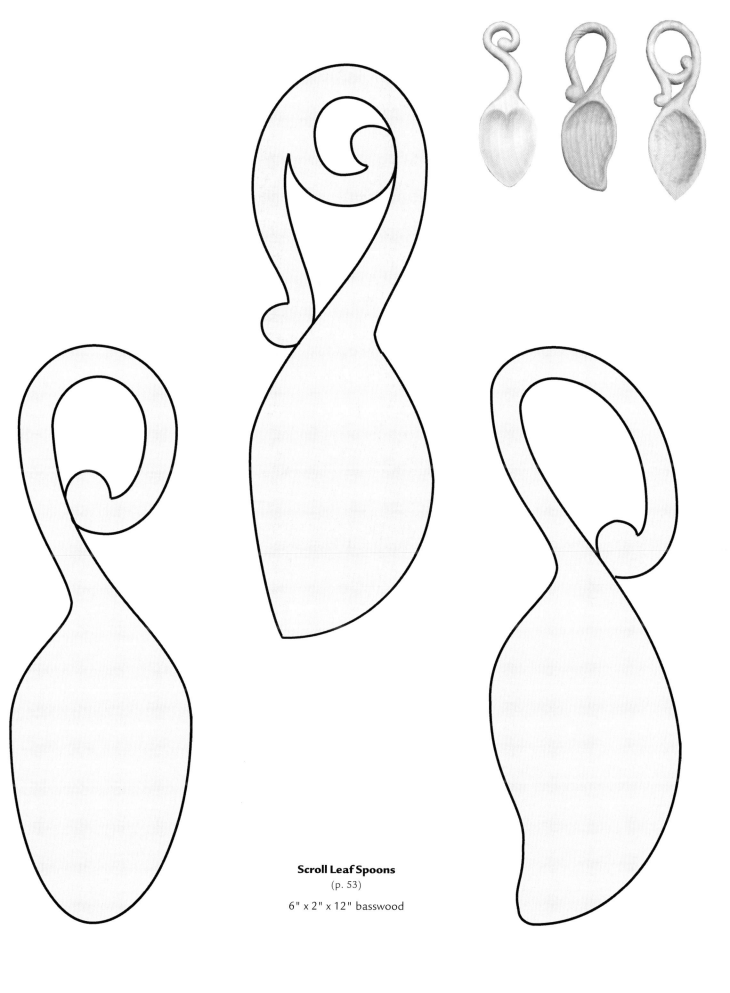

Scroll Leaf Spoons
(p. 53)

6" x 2" x 12" basswood

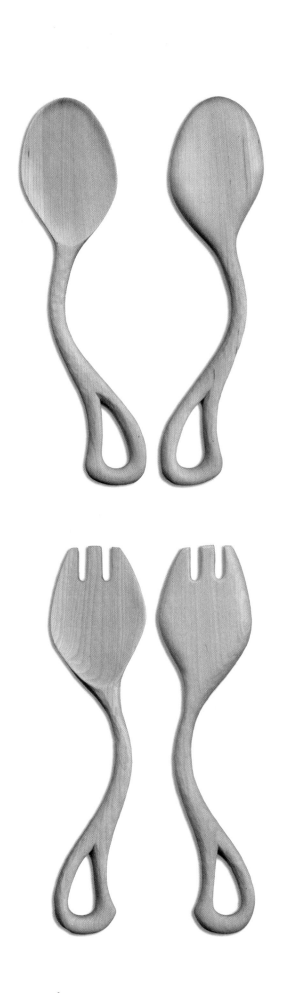

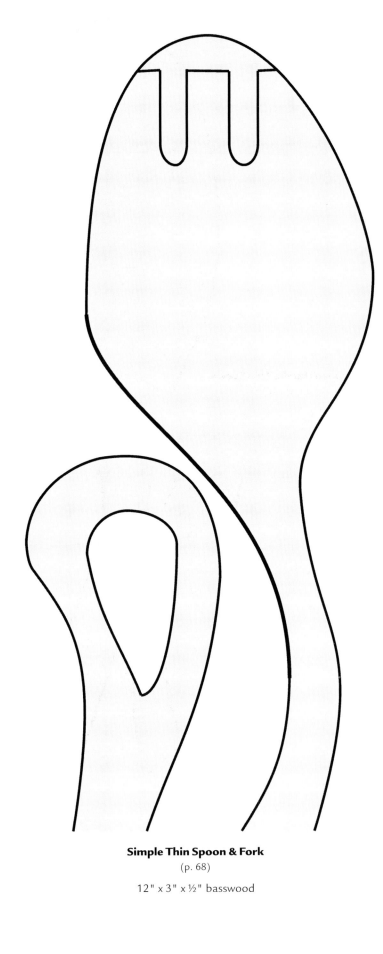

Simple Thin Spoon & Fork
(p. 68)

12" x 3" x ½" basswood

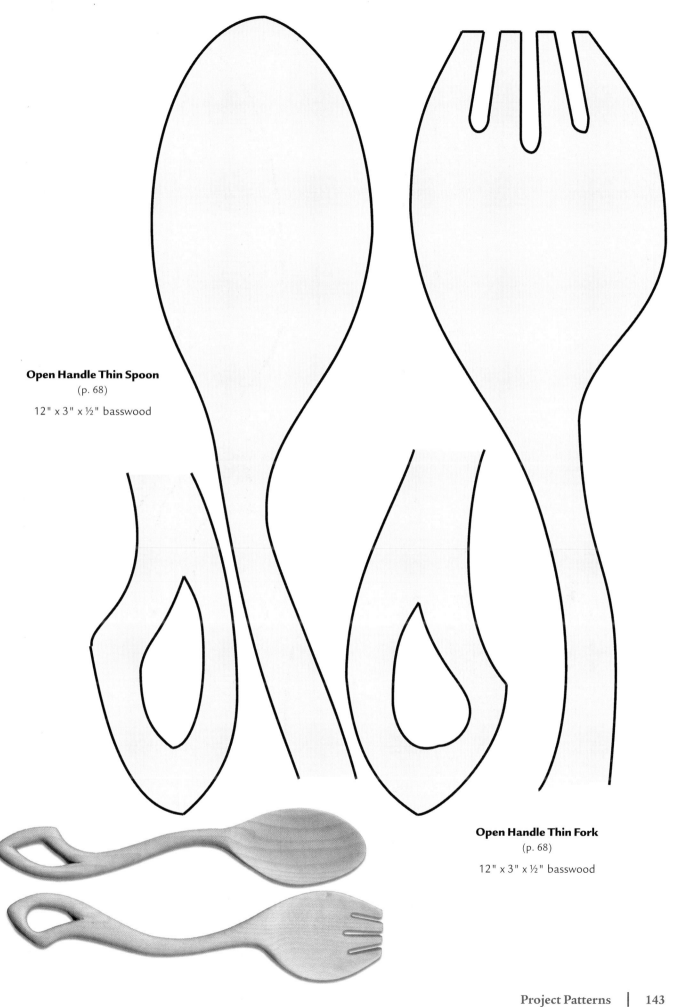

Open Handle Thin Spoon
(p. 68)

12" x 3" x ½" basswood

Open Handle Thin Fork
(p. 68)

12" x 3" x ½" basswood

Pyrography Slotted Spoon
(p. 77)

12" x 3" x ⅕" basswood

Pyrography Spoon
(p. 77)

12" x 3" x ⅕" basswood

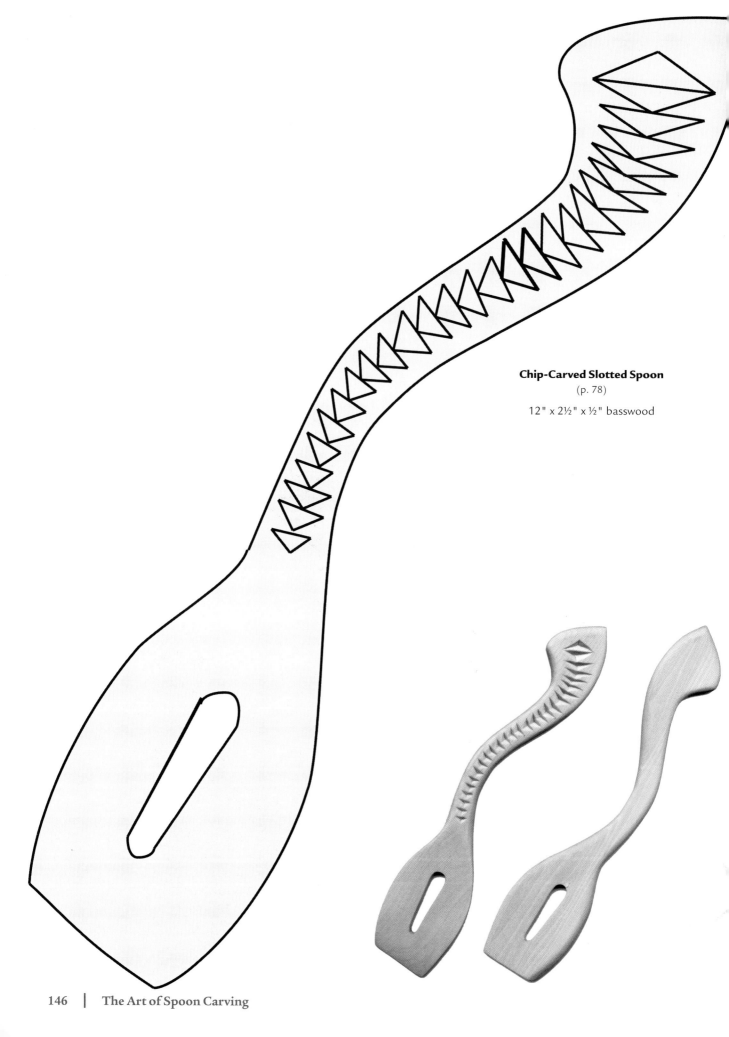

Chip-Carved Slotted Spoon
(p. 78)

12" x 2½" x ½" basswood

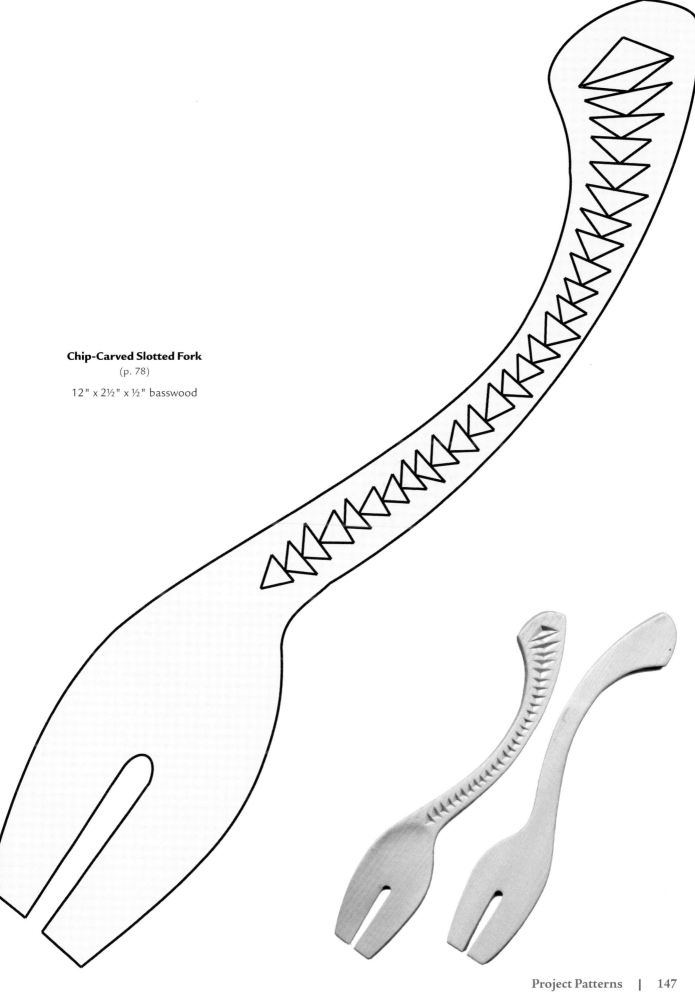

Chip-Carved Slotted Fork
(p. 78)

12" x 2½" x ½" basswood

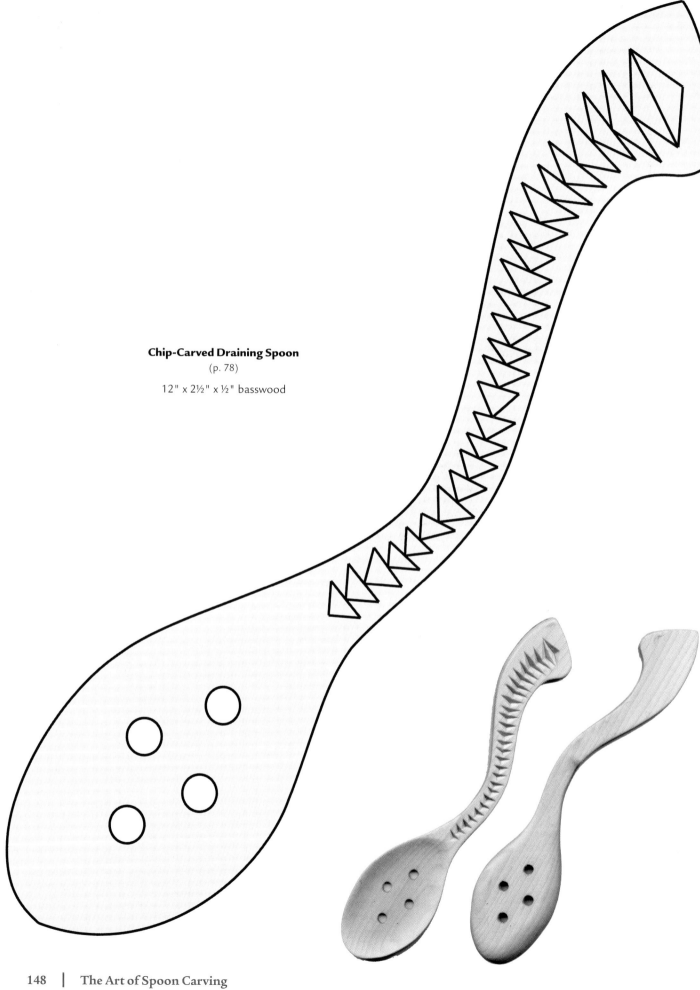

Chip-Carved Draining Spoon
(p. 78)

12" x 2½" x ½" basswood

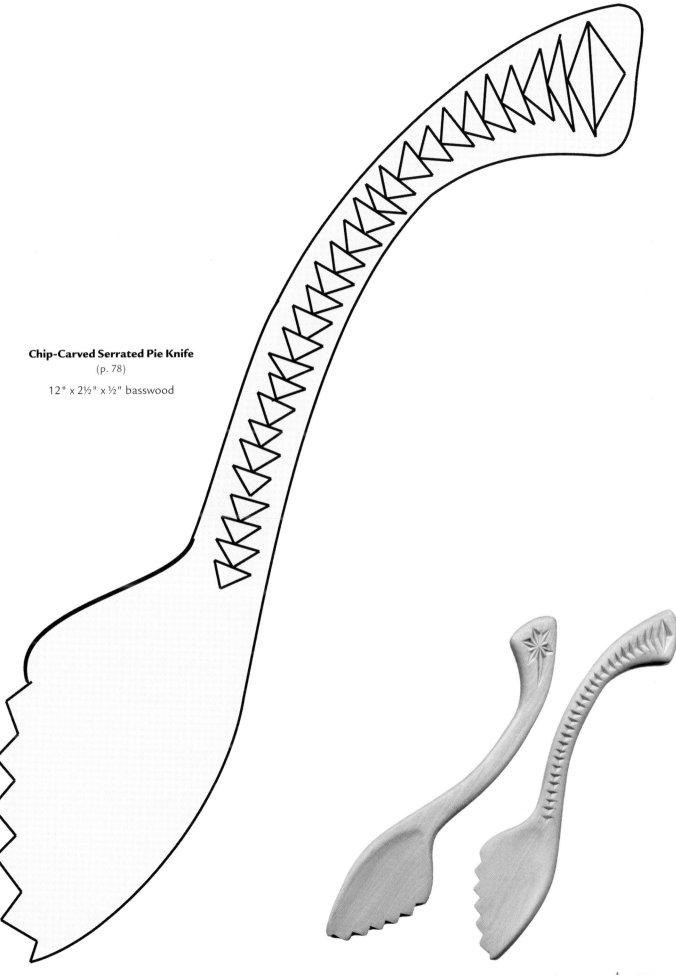

Chip-Carved Serrated Pie Knife
(p. 78)

12" x 2½" x ½" basswood

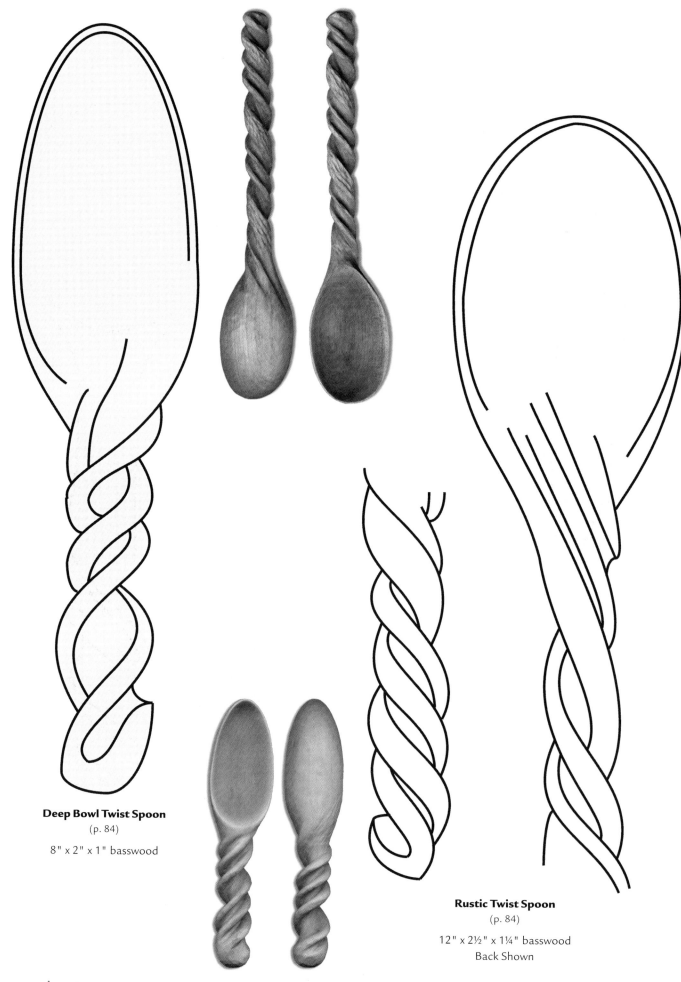

Deep Bowl Twist Spoon
(p. 84)

8" x 2" x 1" basswood

Rustic Twist Spoon
(p. 84)

12" x 2½" x 1¼" basswood
Back Shown

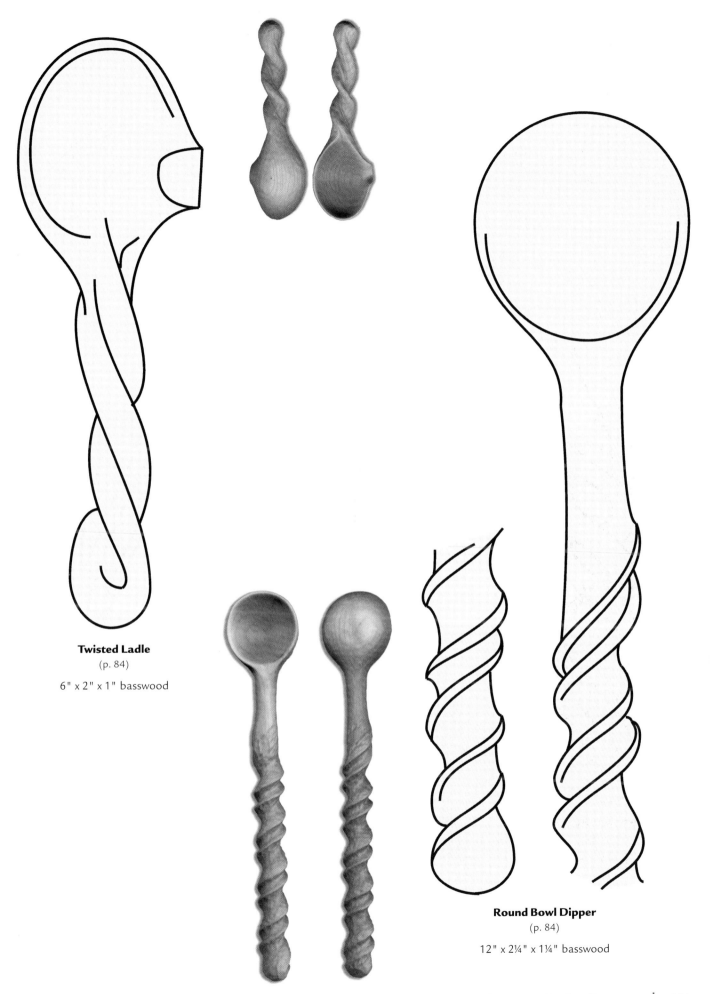

Twisted Ladle
(p. 84)

6" x 2" x 1" basswood

Round Bowl Dipper
(p. 84)

12" x 2¼" x 1¼" basswood

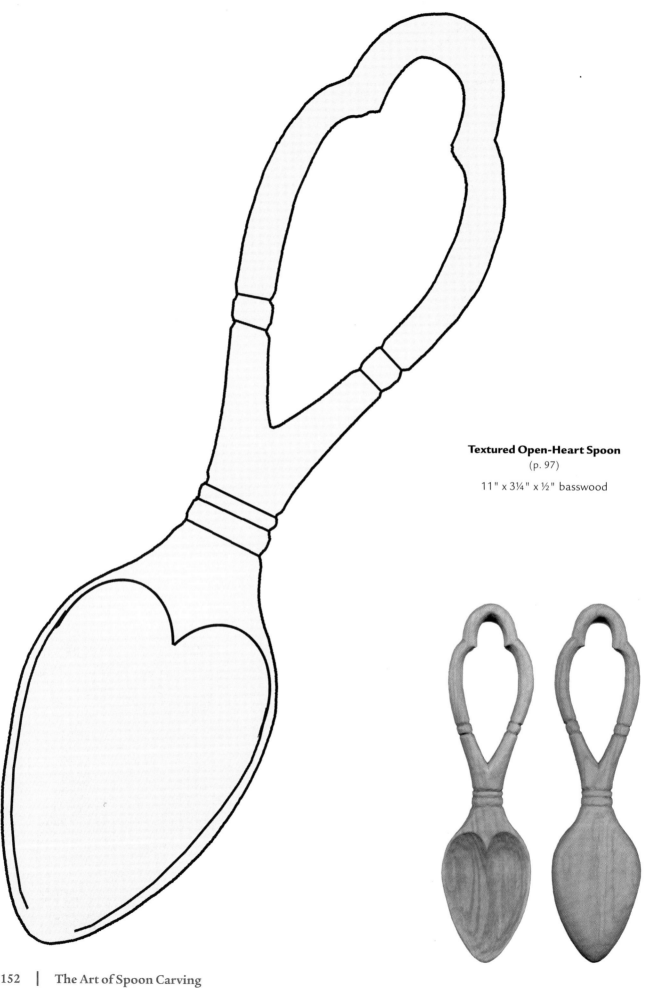

Textured Open-Heart Spoon
(p. 97)

11" x 3¼" x ½" basswood

Heart Strainer
(p. 97)

9½" x 3¼" x 1"

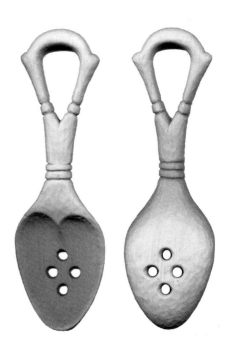

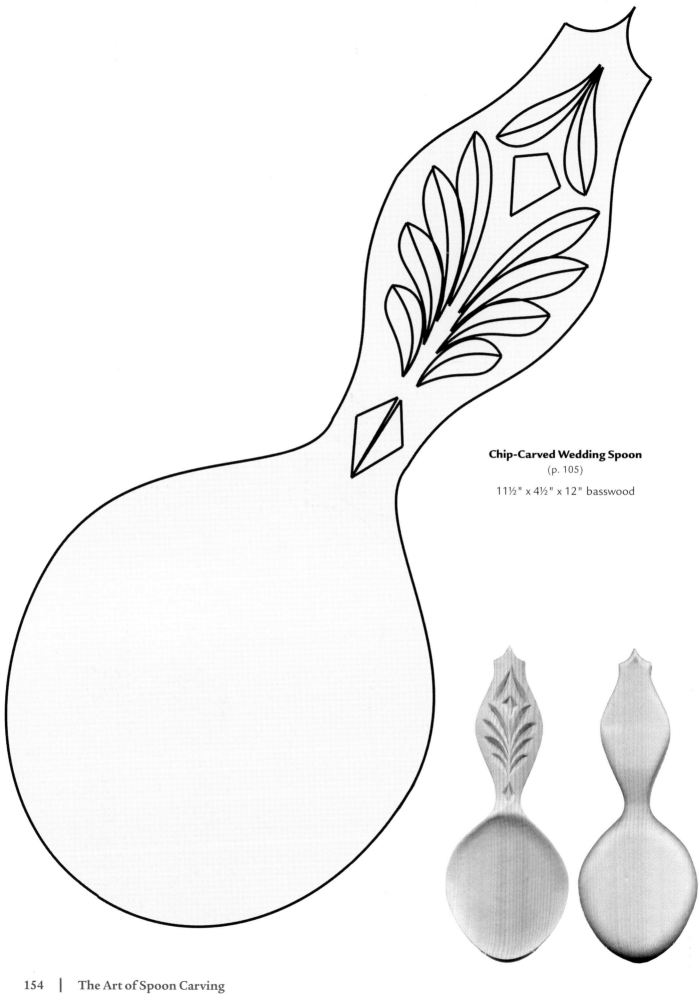

Chip-Carved Wedding Spoon
(p. 105)

11½" x 4½" x 12" basswood

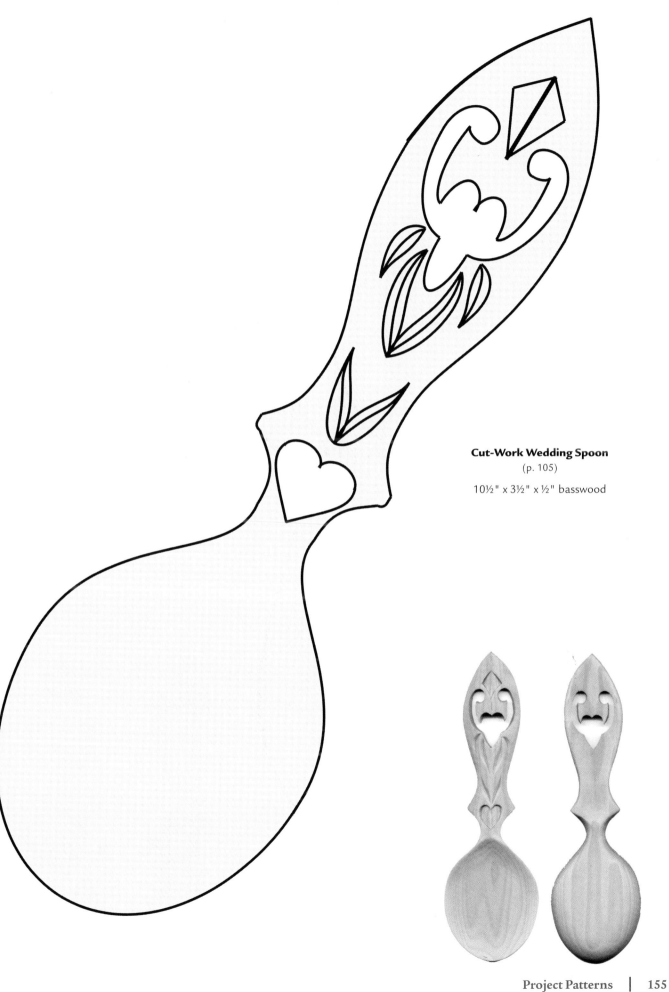

Cut-Work Wedding Spoon
(p. 105)

10½" x 3½" x ½" basswood

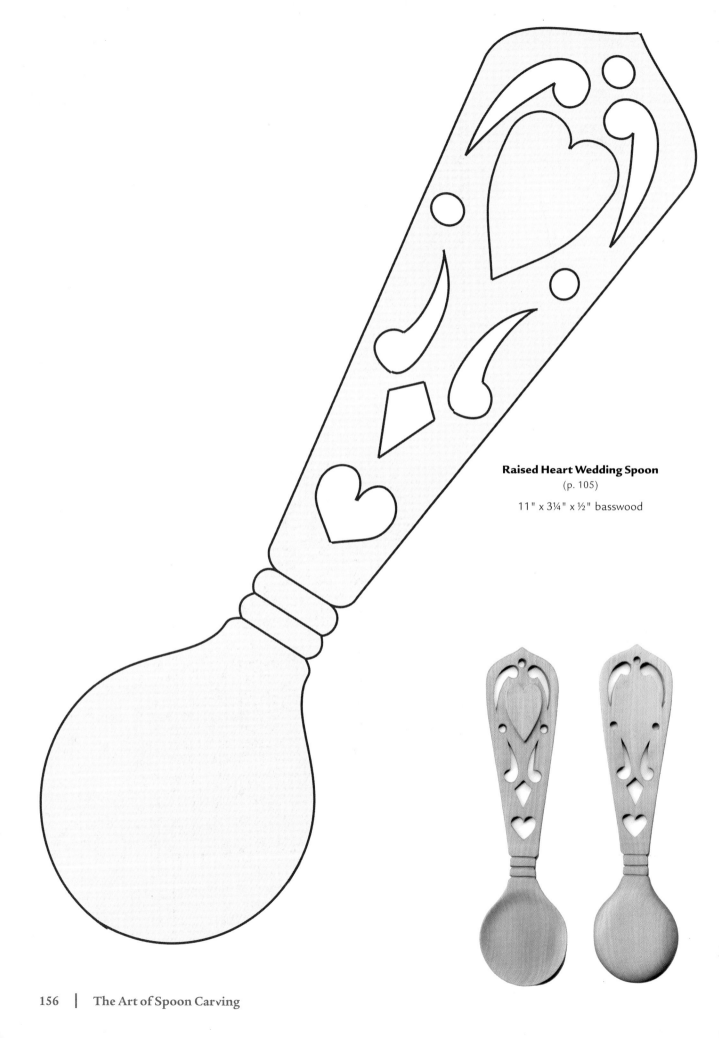

Raised Heart Wedding Spoon
(p. 105)

11" x 3¼" x ½" basswood